Cory Helps Kids Cope with Grief

Playful Activities for Young Children

Liana Lowenstein

Champion Press
Toronto

Copyright © 2024 by Champion Press. All rights reserved.

All rights reserved. Except as indicated, no part of this book may be reproduced, stored in a retrieval system, or transmitted, in any form or by any means, electronic, mechanical, photocopying, microfilming, recording, or otherwise, without express written permission of the author.

Worksheets may be reproduced only within the confines of the use with clients. This limited permission does not grant other rights, nor does it give permission for commercial, resale, syndication, or any other use not contained above. Any other use, or reproduction, is a violation of international laws and is forbidden without express permission from the author.

Library and Archives Canada Cataloguing in Publication

Title: Cory helps kids cope with grief: playful activities for young children / Liana Lowenstein.
Names: Lowenstein, Liana, 1965- author.
Description: Includes bibliographical references.
Identifiers: Canadiana 20230554334 | ISBN 9780995172524 (softcover)
Subjects: LCSH: Grief in children. | LCSH: Children and death. | LCSH: Children—Counseling of.
Classification: LCC BF723.G75 L69 2024 | DDC 155.9/37083—dc23

Published by Champion Press Books: (Telephone) 416-575-7836 www.lianalowenstein.com

About the Author

Liana Lowenstein, MSW, RSW, CPT-S, is a Registered Social Worker, Certified TF-CBT Therapist, and Certified Play Therapist-Supervisor who has been working with children and their families in Toronto since 1988. She provides clinical consultation to mental health practitioners and presents trainings across North America and abroad. She is the founder of Champion Press Publishing Company and has authored numerous publications, which are used by mental health professionals all over the world. She is the winner of the Monica Hubert award for outstanding contribution to play therapy in Canada.

Also from Liana Lowenstein

Paper Dolls and Paper Airplanes:
Therapeutic Exercises for Sexually Traumatized Children
(Co-authored with Geraldine Crisci & Marilyn Lay)

Creative Interventions for Troubled Children and Youth

More Creative Interventions for Troubled Children & Youth

Creative Interventions for Bereaved Children

Creative Interventions for Children of Divorce

Creative Interventions for Children with Anxiety

Assessment and Treatment Techniques for Children, Adolescents, and Families:
Practitioners Share Their Most Effective Techniques (Volumes One through Four)

Creative Family Therapy Techniques:
Play, Art, and Expressive Therapies to Engage Children in Family Sessions

Cory Helps Kids Cope with Divorce:
Playful Therapeutic Activities for Young Children

Cory Helps Kids Cope with Sexual Abuse:
Playful Activities for Traumatized Children

For more information on these books and forthcoming publications, go to the author's website:
www.lianalowenstein.com

Table of Contents

Activities at a Glance	VI
Acknowledgments	VII
Introduction and Theoretical Overview	IX
Getting to Know You	21
Learning about Death	27
Feelings	49
Feelings and Reactions about the Death	53
Telling the Story	59
Helpful Talk	67
Memories	73
Wishes	79
Coping with Hard Days	83
Saying Goodbye	87
Appendix A: Caregiver Questionnaire	93
Appendix B: Family Assessment Activity: Playdough Adventure	99
Appendix C: Welcome Letter for the Child's First Session	100
Appendix D: Child Assessment Activities	101
Appendix E: Cookie Jar	105
References	106
Organizations and Resources	110
Bonus Gift	111

Activities at a Glance

Each chapter contains Cory's Story and activities. If the story seems inappropriate to the child's situation, the activities can be used without the story. The activities can be integrated into individual or family sessions and in grief support groups. Below is a list of the activities and their goals:

NAME OF ACTIVITY	PAGE #	GOALS
Yes, No Game	24	Become better acquainted
Robot-Ragdoll	24	Use muscular relaxation when distressed
Crumpled Paper Throw Game (Psychoeducation version)	29	Acquire knowledge about death related concepts
Guess Which Hand Game	50	Recognize and verbalize a range of emotions
Pillow Talk (Parenting technique)	52	Increase open communication between child and caregiver
Stop! Freeze! Cookie Breathe!	55	Use deep breathing when distressed
Brag Book (Parenting technique)	58	Improve child's behavior and self-esteem
Telling the Story (For traumatic grief)	64	Minimize intrusive and upsetting trauma-related imagery
Helpful Talk Puppets	68	Replace maladaptive cognitions with adaptive ones
Dice Game	76	Preserve positive memories of the deceased
Always in My Heart	76	Transform the relationship with the deceased from one of interaction to one of memory
Magic Carpet Ride	80	Accept the finality of the death
Build-A-Teddy Bear Puzzle	84	Cope with grief bursts
Crumpled Paper Throw Game (Termination version)	89	Review what was learned in sessions
Goodbye Hand	90	Experience a positive termination
Caregiver Questionnaire	93	Gather assessment information
Playdough Adventure	99	Gather family assessment information
Welcome Letter	100	Normalize grief and understand the format of sessions
Red or Black Card Game	101	Gather grief-specific information
Get Moving Grab Bag	102	Channel anxious energy into a positive outlet
People in My World	103	Assess family and community relationships and primary emotions
Cookie Jar	105	Prepare the child for termination

Acknowledgments

I extend my heartfelt thanks, first and foremost, to the remarkable children and parents with whom I have had the privilege of working over the years. They are the true inspiration for this book, imparting important lessons through their resilience and strength.

I am deeply indebted to the following individuals who graciously dedicated their time and expertise to review my manuscript, offering invaluable insights and thoughtful suggestions: Carrie Arnold, Kate Drewry, Linda Goldman, Roy Van Tassel, Andrea Warnick, and Christina Watts-Figueroa. They have played a pivotal role in shaping this publication.

I extend warm appreciation to Dawn Hunter and Katy Delagardelle for their meticulous editorial assistance, and to Kim Bracic for her creative design work.

Special gratitude to my family and friends for their continued support and encouragement. I am profoundly thankful to my husband, Steven, and my daughter, Jaime, for their enduring love, which has helped fill the void left by my mother's death many years ago.

Introduction and Theoretical Overview

This publication is part of a series of books to help children cope with challenging issues. This version targets children ages 4–8 coping with grief. Children can grieve both death and non-death losses, but for this book, the focus is on grief following the death of an important person. Some activities may be adapted for children experiencing a non-death loss—for example, a parent who is incarcerated, parental military deployment, or placement in out-of-home care.

The book includes a therapeutic story (referred to as *Cory's Story*) and a range of innovative activities to engage children, process their grief, and facilitate skill-building. The story and the activities can be used in a variety of settings, including individual and family sessions and children's grief support groups.

This book reflects contemporary views on death, dying, and grief from a largely Western perspective. It is hoped that readers can integrate this information into their cultural and religious practices.

Childhood Grief

Grief is a normal, emotional response to loss. It involves all aspects of the human experience, including social, emotional, cognitive, behavioral, and spiritual dimensions (Harris & Winokuer, 2016). Bereavement is a life event involving the loss of a significant person through death (Kaplow, et al., 2023; Stroebe et al., 2008). *Mourning* is taking the internal experience of grief and expressing it. It is the cultural expression of grief, as seen in traditional or creative rituals (Goldman, 2022).

Bereaved children tend to express grief through actions or behaviors rather than through verbalizations. Some factors that may impact the child's grief reactions include their age and stage; their capacity to understand death; their emotional well-being before the death; the relationship with the person who died; the circumstances surrounding the death; support systems; family dynamics and responses to the death; the family's religious, spiritual, and cultural discourses about the death; cognitive frameworks including self-blame; and previous life experiences (Treisman, 2021). The death can produce emotional, psychological, and neurobiological reactions, including stomach aches, social withdrawal, aggression, difficulty concentrating, regression, eating issues, sleep disturbance, and sad, angry, guilty, hopeless, or anxious feelings. They may develop magical thinking (the belief that their thoughts or actions caused the death), a fearful preoccupation that others will die, or separation anxiety. In children, intense sadness or emotional pain may emerge intermittently. Anger related to the death may be exhibited as irritability, protest behavior, tantrums, aggressiveness, or oppositional behavior (Arnold, 2018; Treisman, 2021).

When children experience the death of a significant person, it is expected and natural that they will experience a range of emotions. The distressing emotions associated with the death tend to decrease over time and come in waves that are often linked to reminders of the person who died. The sadness is interspersed with positive memories of the deceased (Cohen et al., 2017). While the process of grief can be difficult, and the child's life will be forever impacted by the death, most children grieve adaptively and maintain their usual daily functioning across life domains (Kaplow et al., 2010; Keyes et al., 2014). Eventually, the child will accept the reality of the death, process the emotional and cognitive aspects of grief, accomplish the tasks of mourning, and progress through a healthy developmental trajectory (Pearlman et al., 2014).

Though not typical, some children develop grief responses that are more long-lasting, severe, and impairing. These responses involve an extended period of debilitating longing for and/or preoccupation with the person who died, with thoughts or memories of the person who died, or with the circumstances of the death (Van Dijk et al., 2023). Views differ in the field regarding how to conceptualize and intervene when complications significantly impact the grieving process. In 2022, prolonged grief disorder (PGD) was formally included in the DSM-5-TR (*Diagnostic and Statistical Manual of Mental Disorders*, 5th Edition, Text Revision; American Psychiatric Association, 2022) and in the ICD-11 (*International Classification of Diseases*, 11th Revision).

The inclusion of PGD in the DSM-5-TR and ICD-11 has been a topic of debate. Some argue that it leads to improved identification and specialized care and provides mental health professionals with guidance on how to assess and treat individuals who meet the criteria. Others contend that it pathologizes normal grief experiences and can lead to misdiagnosis, and that labeling prolonged grief as a mental disorder stigmatizes individuals who are grieving. As well, grief reactions are highly individual and can vary widely. Some assert that PGD and the post-death time frame for diagnostic consideration are social constructs that cannot be scientifically validated.

Regardless of whether one supports the terminology and inclusion of PGD in the DSM-5-TR and ICD-11, the diagnostic criteria does not apply to young children. Therefore, when supporting young grievers, pay attention to signs that they may be struggling to cope with the death, such as significant changes in behavior, ongoing emotional distress, sleep disturbance, regression in developmental milestones, and refusal to accept the death. If this persists over an extended period and significantly impacts the child's well-being and daily functioning, then an appropriate support plan should be put in place. Keep in mind that longer grief responses can be indicative of many factors, including other losses, familial challenges such as insecure attachment, violence, abuse, and poverty.

Some children, notably after deaths associated with intense fear, helplessness, shock, or horror, develop trauma responses, commonly referred to in the literature as *childhood traumatic grief* (CTG). Traumatic grief in children can occur following sudden, unexpected, violent, gory, or accidental deaths, such as those from a car accident, homicide, suicide, natural disaster, war, or mass violence. Children can also develop traumatic grief when the death was anticipated (e.g., due to illness), and the child felt helpless and saw the person suffering. The child does not have to witness the death directly for it to be traumatic (Cohen et al., 2017).

Whether a child "perceives a loss as traumatic seems to be more subjective and based on the child's experience, than objectively related to categorization of cause of death" (Salloum, 2015, p. 1). Schuurman and DeCristofaro (2010) emphasize that it is the child's perception of a loss, and not the nature of the loss itself, that determines whether a loss is traumatic. The Substance Abuse and Mental Health Services Administration (SAMHSA, 2014) advises that one must experience an event or a set of circumstances as harmful or life-threatening before identifying it as traumatic.

Risk factors that may lead to a child experiencing traumatic grief include the relationship with the deceased; the surviving parent's support of the child; sudden death; the child's level of functioning and coping; beliefs about themselves and the world; and the presence or absence of a supportive, non-stressful environment (Salloum, 2015).

In cases of traumatic grief, children develop death-related trauma responses. Trauma responses interfere with the child's grieving process because they are stuck on the traumatic or horrifying aspects of the death and are unable to endure the thoughts, feelings, and memories necessary for mourning (Cohen et al., 2017; Pearlman et al., 2014).

Cohen and Mannarino (2011) outline the core features of CTG:

- *Reexperiencing*: Frightening or distressing thoughts and images, memories, or dreams of the person, the way the person died, or other situations that seem unrelated to the death. It can also be a cognitive image the child has created and assumes to be true or a false belief, such as imagining the way the person suffered. The child might be distracted by these intrusive thoughts, beliefs, images, or memories.

- *Avoidance*: Avoids thinking or talking about the person who died, even positive memories, because they may lead to scary images of the way that person died. Avoidance or numbing may be expressed by withdrawal or by acting as if they are not upset.

- *Hyperarousal*: Irritability, anger outbursts, trouble sleeping, decreased concentration, increased vigilance and jumpiness, and fears about safety for themself or others.

- *Emotional deregulation:* Difficulty modulating feelings and/or behaviors, especially when reminded of the death. For example, the child may be more irritable and have frequent emotional outbursts.

Additional trauma-related responses may include "the development of irrational fears or phobias, consistent rescue or revenge fantasies, various somatic symptoms that seem to have no medical cause, sudden mood or behavioral changes, or an over-identification with the deceased" (Freedy, 2018, p. 117).

Chronic separation from a caregiver can be experienced by the child as traumatic. They may be sudden, unexpected, and prolonged, and can be accompanied by other stressful events or traumas. Examples of traumatic separation include parental incarceration, immigration, parental deportation, parental military deployment, and placement in out-of-home care. Children who experience traumatic separation may present with posttraumatic responses that are similar to traumatic grief. However, the challenges are different when the caregiver is still alive. For example, the child may hope to be reunited with the caregiver, and this can interfere with their ability to adjust to daily life and to develop healthy coping strategies. As well, the child may mistakenly believe that their absent caregiver abandoned them, think that they caused the caregiver to leave them, or be preoccupied with their caregiver's safety and well-being (National Child Traumatic Stress Network, 2016).

Disenfranchised grief refers to grief that is not openly acknowledged, socially sanctioned, or publicly mourned, often leading to feelings of isolation and confusion (Doka, 1989). Examples of disenfranchised grief in children include the death of an incarcerated parent, the death of a foster parent or foster sibling, suicide, or a substance-related death. In these cases, children's feelings and grief reactions are often overlooked or downplayed, preventing them from receiving the necessary support and validation to cope with their grief effectively. Adults can support bereaved children by opening communication and inviting personal expression, involving them in mourning rituals and commemoration, and validating their experience of grief as genuine and acceptable (Blin & Jonas-Simpson, 2018).

Children's Concept of Death

Past experiences with death, as well as age, emotional and cognitive development, and surroundings, heavily influence a child's concept of death, as do cultural, familial, and individual factors (Goldman, 2022).

Infants have no understanding of the concept of death, but they react to upset and changes in their environment brought about by the absence of a significant caregiver. They will also be impacted by emotional withdrawal that can happen if a main caregiver is bereaved.

Up to the age of 6 months, babies will experience the death of a significant caregiver as a sense of abandonment. From around the age of 8 months, babies begin to develop a mental image of the person who has died and have a sense of missing them.

Preschool-age children are very concrete and egocentric. Death is experienced as a loss of love and protection. The child may feel a sense of abandonment with the death of a primary caregiver. They tend to view death as temporary or reversible, as in cartoons. The child may think that death is like sleep, which can create a fear of sleep and darkness (Goldman, 2014). Most children in this age group do not understand that death is permanent, that everyone and every living thing will eventually die, and that dead things do not eat, sleep, or breathe.

Between the ages of 5 and 8 years, children gradually begin to develop an understanding of death. They may avoid the reality of death. They begin to understand the finality of death but do not understand that it happens to everybody. Children's developmentally normative use of imagination and magical thinking, typically used between the ages of 2 and 7, can mean that some children believe that their thoughts or actions caused the death and/or sadness of those around them. The child may experience feelings of guilt and shame related to the death, or they may believe that the death is punishment for something they did or thought about. For example, if a child's sibling died, they may blame themselves for the death because that morning, they had an argument over a toy (i.e., their negative thoughts caused something "bad" to happen).

While children ages 9 to 12 have the cognitive capacity to understand the finality of death and that death is a part of life, they may still have levels of magical thinking. They may be curious about the physical process of death and what happens after a person dies. They may fear their own death because of uncertainty about what happens after they die. Fear of the unknown, loss of control, and separation from family and friends can be the school-age child's main sources of anxiety related to death.

Through their development, young children may exhibit a wide range of emotional reactions to death, including confusion, fear, curiosity, sadness, and sometimes even indifference. These reactions vary depending on their individual personalities, their past experiences, and the support and guidance they receive from main caregivers.

Culture refers to "the beliefs, attitudes, values (collectivism vs. individualism), behaviors (family roles), and practices (e.g., death rituals) shared by a group to support its survival within various contexts" (Harris & Bordere, 2016, p. 10). Cultural, religious, and family beliefs play an instrumental role in shaping a child's understanding of death.

Providing honest, developmentally appropriate information can help children develop an accurate understanding of death and the coping mechanisms needed to deal with its emotional impact (Warnick, 2015). The chapter "Learning about Death" provides psychoeducation in an engaging format for children and offers guidance on how caregivers can accurately explain death in a manner that aligns with the child's understanding, personality, and stage of development.

Rapport-Building and Assessment

Not all bereaved children require professional support. Many children will address grief without specialized services. In some situations, offering psychoeducation to caregivers is the most useful approach so that they can provide daily support to their child. There are some indicators for when professional support is recommended (e.g., when children display more impairing emotional responses or traumatic grief). The professional must complete a careful and thorough screening and create a grief support plan.

When children and families are accessing professional support, an atmosphere of safety must be created in which the child and caregivers feel accepted, understood, and respected. Developing rapport "consists of being warm, open, and curious, and this therapeutic imperative holds across contexts, modalities, and presenting concerns" (Rabenstein, 2018, p. 24). Connecting in a positive way with children "is shaped by who we are more than what we do. In our various roles as adults, maintaining an open, warm, and nonjudgmental attitude conveys safety and a sense of acceptance, which is particularly important for bereaved youth" (Arnold, 2018, p. 14). Developing a positive relationship with children and their caregivers leads to a deeper and more significant level of sharing in sessions.

It is essential to engage the child and family in the assessment and work collaboratively with the caregiver on the support plan. A comprehensive assessment should cover the following areas:

- Caregiver's history and prior exposure to trauma and loss
- Child's history and prior exposure to trauma and loss
- Child and family functioning before and after the death
- Child's strengths, protective qualities, skills, and interests
- Child's relationships with family and peers
- Child's academic, emotional, and behavioral functioning at school
- Child's relationship with the person who died
- Circumstances of the death
- Caregiver's strengths and vulnerabilities in caring for the child
- Caregiver's beliefs about what the child should be told about the death and how the death was communicated to the child
- Current family dynamics, responses to the death, and daily functioning and routine
- Specific religious, cultural, spiritual, and family beliefs and traditions regarding death and mourning
- Child's involvement in mourning rituals and the goodbye process
- Child's grief reactions, indicators of trauma, and coping styles
- Family's grief reactions and ability to communicate openly about the death
- Continuity versus disruption of the child's daily routines, changes in who provides direct care for the child
- Secondary losses (e.g., moving, changing schools)
- Legal, criminal, or financial issues that have occurred since the death
- Community supports
- Caregiver's willingness to fully participate in sessions
- Other major stressors the child or family is experiencing

All primary caregivers should be interviewed as part of the assessment process. The first face-to-face session with the caregivers is critical as it sets the tone for ongoing work. The focus of this initial session is on developing a positive rapport; gathering relevant information on the child, caregiver, and the family; highlighting the importance of the caregiver's role in supporting their child and encouraging their involvement in sessions; and instilling a sense of hope regarding the child's adjustment to the death.

A Caregiver Questionnaire is included in Appendix A. The information in the questionnaire is best collected via a face-to-face interview with the caregivers. This facilitates rapport-building and elicits more detailed information than caregivers might offer if they were to complete it on their own. Gathering detailed information regarding the circumstances of the death can be a sensitive issue as it evokes emotionally laden feelings for the caregivers. Therefore, before delving into details related to the death, a supportive, non-judgmental atmosphere must be created.

The caregiver's ability to help their child cope with the death is inextricably tied to their own history of trauma and loss (Lieberman et al., 2005). Therefore, as part of the assessment, be sure to collect background information on the primary caregivers. The Caregiver Questionnaire in Appendix A includes questions pertaining to the caregiver's history.

The caregiver may also be experiencing varying levels of trauma responses or traumatic grief. Because of the significant impact this can have on the child, it is important to assess the caregiver's grief responses.

The child's grief reactions must be assessed to determine whether specific trauma-focused treatment is indicated. The conceptualization of childhood traumatic grief requires that (1) the person died under circumstances the child perceives as traumatic; (2) the child is experiencing significant indicators of posttraumatic stress disorder (reexperiencing, avoidance, hyperarousal, emotional deregulation); and (3) the grief responses substantially interfere with the child's functioning (Cohen et al., 2017).

Appendix D presents assessment interventions for use with the child. The Red or Black Card Game assesses thoughts and feelings related to the death. People in My World assesses family and community relationships and available supports. This activity also evaluates such feelings as sadness, fear, and self-blame. The child is prompted to include self, significant family and community members (both positive and negative relationships) so that these relationships can be assessed.

When children attend a first session, they may feel confused about why they are there and nervous about what to expect. The Welcome Letter (Appendix C) engages the child, normalizes feelings, and explains the format of sessions. The letter can be modified to suit the child's age and circumstances.

A thorough assessment should include observation of the child within the context of their family. Playdough Adventure (Appendix B) is a family assessment technique that evaluates family dynamics including roles, hierarchy, communication patterns, and problem-solving.

Collecting information from multiple sources leads to a more accurate and comprehensive assessment. Therefore, in addition to meeting with the caregivers and the child, it may be helpful to collect information from the child's teacher and any previous professionals. Validated screening tools for the caregiver to complete about the child can also provide valuable information on grief/trauma responses and other developmental, social, emotional, and behavioral issues.

After the assessment has been completed, it is essential to provide feedback to the caregivers. When describing the assessment findings, it is best to begin by highlighting the strengths of the child, the caregivers, and the family relationships. It is also important to communicate, in a sensitive manner, the areas requiring further support.

The caregivers should be involved in setting and prioritizing goals for sessions. During the feedback meeting, emphasize the critical role of caregivers, highlighting how their involvement and support may be the most important factor in their child's adjustment to the death.

If the caregiver is struggling with their own grief, parenting, or other issues, and is not receiving support services, then the feedback session is an appropriate time to discuss referrals. Ensuring that the caregiver receives the help that they need will optimize their capacity to support their child.

Grief-Focused Intervention

Although each child's circumstances are unique, there are typical tasks of grieving to accomplish (Cohen et al., 2017; Worden, 1996):

- Accept the reality and permanence of the death
- Build skills for coping that promote healing and well-being
- Experience and cope with the painful emotions of the death
- Adjust to life changes that result from the death
- Resolve any ambivalent feelings toward the deceased and preserve positive memories of the person who died
- Maintain an appropriate, continuous bond to the person who died
- Develop new relationships and deepen existing relationships
- Prepare for future loss reminders and setbacks

While these tasks are typically addressed in grief work, keep in mind that each child's grieving process is unique, and intervention should be tailored to the developmental level of the child, as well as the family, cultural, spiritual, and religious customs of the child (Freedy, 2018).

When considering grief-focused intervention, distinguish between children for whom supportive grief work is sufficient (such as a children's support group) and children who may need specialized therapeutic services. This determination must be based on an understanding of the child's grief responses, as noted above.

Children's grief support groups and grief therapy are both valuable resources for children who are coping with the death of a significant person, but they serve different purposes and have distinct approaches. Children's grief support groups bring together children who have experienced similar losses. The group provides an opportunity for children to share their feelings and experiences with others who understand what they are going through. This helps children feel less alone in their grief. Support groups are typically led by trained facilitators who may have personal experience with grief. While the group facilitators implement grief-specific activities and provide guidance and structure, they are not necessarily trained professionals. Grief therapy involves sessions with a trained professional, and the treatment plan is tailored to the specific needs of the grieving child.

If the assessment reveals trauma responses (traumatic grief), then the child will benefit from both trauma and grief-focused intervention. Trauma-focused cognitive behavioral therapy (TF-CBT) (Cohen et al., 2017) is an evidence-based model that can be used with traumatically bereaved children as young as three. Trauma-focused components address trauma responses and grief-focused components help the child engage in tasks of grieving. A thorough explanation of TF-CBT is beyond the scope of this text. It is essential to be properly trained in the model before using it.

Creative structured play-based activities, presented within the context of an empathically attuned therapeutic relationship, engage children and enhance the effectiveness of TF-CBT. Blending structured play therapy techniques into TF-CBT allows effective implementation of TF-CBT without changing its theoretical underpinnings. Indeed, "the originators of TF-CBT have encouraged the use of art, games, role plays, music, and playfulness in its implementation" (Cavett & Drewes, 2012, p. 125). Villarreal-Davis et al. (2021) also underscore the benefits of play therapy. Through play therapy, young grievers can safely express and explore their grief-related emotions. The playful techniques presented in this book aim to provide a developmentally appropriate, engaging modality for children and facilitate skill-building.

When trauma and grief responses are both present, it is recommended to partially resolve the trauma issues before addressing the emotions of grief. This is especially applicable when the child is preoccupied with the horrifying aspects of the death. In these cases, children cannot think of positive memories of the person who died because they are stuck on the terrifying aspects or negative thoughts and feelings related to the death. Moreover, traumatically bereaved children typically have avoidance reactions and are so detached from their feelings that they are unable to experience the painful emotions of grief. For these reasons, some trauma-focused activities should be incorporated into the initial sessions, before the grief issues (Cohen et al., 2017).

Prior to introducing CBT-oriented interventions, it is important to enhance a child's ability to self-regulate emotional reactions (Edgar-Bailey & Kress, 2010). Early childhood experiences of trauma affect the development of the brain's lower regulatory areas (brainstem and diencephalons). Perry and Hambrick (2008) suggest the use of somatosensory activities such as soothing music, peaceful imagery, controlled breathing, regulated movement, or yoga.

Neurodivergence refers to an individual who has a less typical (considered "normal" by society) cognitive variation such as autism, ADHD, dyslexia, dyspraxia, dyscalculia, sensory differences, obsessive compulsive disorder (OCD), and Tourette's syndrome. Most neurodivergent children will present with experiencing some level of rejection, being misunderstood, feeling confused, feeling anxious, feeling devalued, having poor self-worth, and being regularly disabled by society and systems (Grant, 2023). When working with neurodivergent children, it is essential to integrate neurodiversity-affirming practices into their bereavement support services. For example, understand and respect their communication styles and sensory sensitivities.

Intervention for bereaved children requires a nuanced understanding, as it does not follow a straightforward path. According to Freedy (2018), the therapeutic journey is characterized by multiple oscillations between each phase, reflecting the dynamic nature of children's grieving processes. As children encounter new developmental stages, they might revisit certain aspects of their grief, requiring adaptive interventions to meet their evolving emotional needs.

Caregiver Involvement and Family Sessions

Whenever possible, the child's primary caregivers should be involved in the sessions. The caregiver may be a parent, stepparent, common-law partner, foster parent, grandparent, or some other adult responsible for the care of the child. Several studies have identified associations between "positive" caregiving behaviors and improved child outcomes following the death of a significant person (Haine et al., 2008; Sandler et al., 2013; Shapiro et al., 2014). These positive caregiver behaviors include (1) engaging in enjoyable family activities that strengthen positive bonds and build family cohesion; (2) enhancing family identity by redefining the relationship to the deceased person; (3) increasing warmth and communication; and (4) maintaining continuity in family routines and activities.

Bereaved children need physical and emotional comfort and reassurance. Their grief reactions must be understood and responded to sensitively, especially since children often externalize their feelings through behavioral issues and emotional dysregulation (Watts-Figueroa & McCallum, 2023). Educating caregivers on being attuned to the child, distinguishing between misbehavior and trauma responses, and disciplining appropriately are important goals (Freedy, 2018).

This book includes letters to be given to the caregiver at each session. These letters provide information so the caregiver can better understand and support their child. Use clinical discretion regarding how to integrate these letters into the intervention process. One option is to give the letters to the caregiver to read while meeting with the child, and then to review the letters during the caregiver's sessions. Another option is to give the letters to the caregiver at the end of the caregiver's session to enhance the learning between sessions.

Coping skills are also important to foster in bereaved children. Assigning homework is one way to facilitate generalization and mastery of skills learned in sessions. Ideally, the coping strategies are taught to both the child and the caregiver so the caregiver can coach the child to practice at home and to apply the techniques to situations outside sessions.

If the person who died was a family member, then the child's caregivers and siblings will be dealing with their own grief issues. Efforts should be made to involve the whole family in sessions. Although the interventions in this book have been developed for individual work with the child, many of the activities can be used in family sessions. Additional interventions for family sessions should focus on opening communication among family members, strengthening family relationships, building empathy and understanding, and enhancing the family's problem-solving abilities. Family interventions that are playful will be more engaging and developmentally appropriate. Refer to these books for further information on family play therapy: *Play in Family Therapy* (Gil, 2015); *Attachment-Focused Family Play Therapy* (Spooner, 2021); *Attachment Centered Play Therapy* (Mellenthin, 2019); *Creative Interventions for Bereaved Children* (Lowenstein, 2006); *Creative Family Therapy Techniques* (Lowenstein, 2010); *Assessment and Treatment Activities for Children, Adolescents, and Families, Volumes One Through Four* (Lowenstein, 2008-2022); *Play Therapy Activities* (LaVigne, 2020); and *Engaging Children in Family Therapy* (Sori, 2006).

Obstacles that may prevent caregiver participation in sessions include caregiver's own grief, caregiver mental illness, scheduling, and lack of childcare or affordable transportation. Make the effort to work through these obstacles and build a strong alliance with the caregiver. Killough-McGuire and McGuire (2001) outline helpful strategies for engaging caregivers:

- Always be respectful.
- Reflect, validate, and empathize with the caregiver's feelings.
- Point out the caregiver's strengths, especially their concern for the child.
- Affirm the caregiver's parenting efforts and progress.
- Explore the caregiver's potential concerns related to differences of culture, gender, religion, or other factors that may make them feel they are not being understood, accepted, or respected.
- Discuss and try to resolve practical barriers to participating in sessions.
- Highlight the importance of the caregiver's role in the child's progress.

Working with Very Young Children

This book is geared to children ages 4-8. Developmentally sensitive adaptations may need to be made to some of the activities. Young children's ability to understand complex issues may be improved by specific approaches, such as using more concrete examples, fewer open-ended questions, and visual cues (Bierman, 1983). Experiential, playful interventions that deemphasize cognitive and verbal skills are indicated (Knell & Dasari, 2006).

Working with young children requires specific knowledge and skills. Below are guidelines for working more effectively with young populations:

- Understand stage-salient developmental issues for preschoolers and young school-age children.
- Be familiar with how children remember (e.g., they can recall certain significant events but not details of time and place; therefore, they may throw in bits from several memories rather than focusing on one memory).
- Be aware that young children may say things in order to please, or they may make up a story or embellish to master an overwhelming experience. This can be addressed by taking a curious stance, validating, and empathizing with the child's feelings.
- Use simple language and speak slowly.
- Present one concept at a time.
- Use shorter session activities to sustain young children's attention.
- Create a short visual schedule that orients children to the session structure and activities, and keep the structure consistent.
- Use repetition in playful, creative ways.
- Take frequent pauses to check for comprehension.
- Enlist caregivers to help young children review and practice new concepts and skills at home.
- Provide the child and their caregiver with handouts to take home that feature visual cues and pictures to enhance skill practice.

Collaborating with School Personnel

Bereaved children may struggle at school. For example, they may have difficulty concentrating or present behavioral difficulties during class. They may talk about the death with their classmates, or they may be reluctant to discuss it at all. Providing the child's school with information on bereaved children allows teachers to respond with greater sensitivity to their students' needs. Handouts to give to school personnel can be found online (e.g., Dougy Center and the National Child Traumatic Stress Network offer free resources). Ongoing communication with the child's teacher is recommended, to provide support, reinforce the child's mastery of skills and concepts, and to track the child's progress.

Religious, Spiritual, and Cultural Beliefs and Mourning Rituals

Families will have specific beliefs about death and will practice certain mourning rituals based on their religion, spiritual, and cultural beliefs. Honor these beliefs and be accepting of diversity. Grief supporters "must be mindful and respectful of the cultural narratives, practices, and responses around death, caring, and health. This includes holding in mind how our own biases, assumptions, beliefs, and attitudes can color these, judge these, and over-identify with them" (Treisman, 2021, p. 199).

Gather information from caregivers about their family's beliefs and mourning rituals, and, where appropriate, integrate it into *Cory's Story* and the activities. The Caregiver Questionnaire in Appendix A includes questions to gather this information. It can also be helpful to speak with religious leaders or others in the community to learn about the family's religious, spiritual, or cultural beliefs and traditions. Identifying information about the child and family should not be disclosed without written permission.

Modeling Open and Direct Communication about Death

Many people find it difficult to talk openly and directly about death. It is essential to model clear and direct language when communicating about death with both children and caregivers. For example, use terms such as *death* and *dying* instead of *passed away* or *loss* or *is gone*. The purposeful use of self-disclosure can be healing for the child. As Goldman (2022) highlights, "our honesty in seeing and relaying loss and grief issues that run through our lives will indeed be the role model for our young people" (p. 9).

Additional Tips and Clinical Guidelines
Below are some practical guidelines for appropriately using this book:

- Each chapter contains *Cory's Story* and activities. Modify the story and activities to suit the developmental, cultural, spiritual, and clinical needs of the child. (Note that the story has been written so it will be appropriate and relevant to a wide variety of situations. However, if adaptations are made to this publication, be sure to maintain the following copyright notice on every page: © Original Copyright Liana Lowenstein 2024; All Rights Reserved.) If the story seems inappropriate to the child's situation, the activities can be used without the story.

- Gather required materials before each session (see the materials list at the beginning of each chapter).

- Copy the story and the letters for the caregiver. **(The book may be reproduced for direct use with children and their caregivers. Any other use or reproduction is a violation of international copyright laws.)**

- Place the child's copy of *Cory's Story* in a scrapbook and keep it in a locked storage unit until the last session, at which point, if appropriate, it can be given to the caregiver to keep in a safe, private place for their child to look through in the future.

- Read one chapter of *Cory's Story* to the child each session. Provide the caregiver with a copy of the chapter and the corresponding letter to read and process with them during their individual session. While there is some flexibility with the order in which the chapters are used, the issues addressed in each chapter do follow a particular sequence. For instance, essential skills are taught in beginning chapters so that the child can draw on these skills in subsequent sessions.

- Cory is presented as gender-neutral so that children of any gender identity can relate. Therefore, refer to Cory using the child's preferred pronouns.

- Write the child's responses to each question in the space provided. Offer the child assorted colored pencils or fine-tip markers so they can choose a "color of the day" for their responses.

- Follow the same structure in every session to help the child become comfortable with the predictability of the process. Begin each session with a brief engagement activity. (Many books outline play-based engagement activities.) Next, guide the child through a relaxation exercise or short mindfulness video on YouTube. Once the child is relaxed, read a chapter of *Cory's Story* and complete the chapter's activities. Devote the last part of the session to child-led play or to a fun activity.

- If the caregiver is not part of the session, then they can be invited in at the end (or a brief phone or virtual meeting can be scheduled) to provide feedback on the child's session, review skills learned, and discuss implementation of the homework.

- Prepare the child well in advance of the last session. The Cookie Jar activity (Appendix E) is geared especially to young children to help prepare them. It should be introduced when the child has five sessions left.

This publication has been specifically designed to engage bereaved children and to help them approach their grief within the context of a supportive environment. It is hoped that this book will help children safely and playfully navigate through their grief journey.

Chapter Overview
Getting to Know You

Goals
- Become better acquainted
- Identify with Cory to reduce feelings of isolation
- Increase open communication
- Learn and implement healthy coping skills

Materials
- Scrapbook to hold the child's copy of Cory's Story, as well as other activities completed in sessions
- Markers or colored pencils
- Camera (optional)
- Two copies of "Getting to Know You" (one copy for the child's scrapbook, one copy for the caregiver)
- Letter for the caregiver

Guidelines and Process Issues

The focus of the first chapter of *Cory's Story* is on fostering rapport. The importance of building a positive relationship cannot be overemphasized. Children who are dealing with a significant death often struggle with trust and may have heightened anxiety. A warm, accepting environment will allow children to more readily engage in sessions.

Cory's Story can be a helpful tool to facilitate engagement. This chapter introduces Cory (the main character) to the child. Through the story, the child realizes that they are not alone—that there are other grieving children.

Cory's Story can be introduced as follows: "Today we're going to begin reading *Cory's Story*. This is a story about a child who is kind of like you. Each time you come here, we'll read a new chapter of *Cory's Story*. There are questions about the story for you to answer, so you get to participate. Let's begin the story!"

The Yes, No Game provides an engaging way to build rapport. Since the game does not require the child to talk, it is an especially appropriate activity to use with children who are highly anxious, shy, or quiet. If the child seems ready, then open-ended follow-up questions that require a verbal answer can be asked. For example, if the child nods yes to the question "Do you have any pets?" then a follow-up question can be "What kind of pet do you have?"

Teaching coping skills is an essential element in grief work. In this session, the child learns Robot-Ragdoll, a progressive muscle relaxation strategy. This technique helps the child learn the difference between muscular tension and relaxation, and how to control muscle tension in their own body. This relaxation strategy is particularly helpful for children who are hypervigilant, have difficulty falling asleep, or have somatic reactions. The caregiver should learn Robot-Ragdoll as well so they can practice alongside the child each night.

Take a picture of the child in the first session to put on the cover of their scrapbook. This personalizes the scrapbook and serves as a visual reminder for the child in later years when they are looking through their scrapbook.

Some children, especially those who have endured multiple losses or traumas, will need additional sessions devoted specifically to building engagement. While the engagement process goes beyond simply using a game or an activity, playful techniques help create a positive environment for young children. A wide variety of creative engagement techniques are available in the literature.

Fostering a positive relationship with the caregiver is vital to maximizing the child's progress. The session with the caregiver, then, is an important component of the engagement phase.

Getting to Know You

This is a story about a child named Cory. Something very sad happened to Cory. Someone died. The person who died was important to Cory. Cory has a lot of upset, mixed-up feelings about what happened. But we'll talk more about that later. Let's find out more about Cory. Cory loves to play at the park, watch TV, and color. Cory loves pizza, chocolate, and broccoli—yup, that's right. Cory loves broccoli!

What is the name of the child in this story?

What is your name?

Cory loves to play at the park, watch TV, and color. What are some of your favorite things to do?

Cory loves pizza, chocolate, and broccoli. What are some of your favorite foods?

Did someone die who was important to Cory?

Who is the person who died who was important to you?

Cory went to see someone named Ana. Ana is a feelings helper. That means Ana's job is to help children learn ways to cope with upset feelings.

What is the name of Cory's feelings helper?

What is the name of your feelings helper? (Hint: The person reading this story with you.)

Does a feelings helper help children learn ways to cope with upset feelings?

Ana said, "Let's play a game so I can get to know you. It's called the Yes, No Game."

Let's play the Yes, No Game too! It will be a fun way for me to get to know you.

Yes, No Game
I'm going to ask you some questions to get to know you. If your answer to the question is yes, then move your head up and down like this (demonstrate what nodding looks like). If your answer to the question is no, then shake your head side to side like this (demonstrate what shaking head looks like).

Questions for the Yes, No Game
1. Do you like ice cream?
2. Do you like playing at the park?
3. Do you have purple hair?
4. Do you like to color or do art?
5. Have you ever been on an airplane?
6. Are you 400 years old?
7. Do you have any pets?
8. Do you like to go swimming?
9. Are there any foods you really, really hate?
10. Do you like to watch TV?

(Read after playing the Yes, No Game.)
Ana explained, "When children are dealing with the death of an important person, they have a lot of mixed-up feelings. But you are getting help now so you can learn ways to feel better. One way to feel better is to do Robot-Ragdoll to relax your body."

Ana showed Cory how to do Robot-Ragdoll. You can learn it too! Let's follow the instructions to learn how to do Robot-Ragdoll.

Robot-Ragdoll
Step 1: Stand up straight and stiff like a robot. Make all the muscles in your body from your head to your toes go tight (Not too tight—it shouldn't hurt!). Keep your body tight like a robot for five seconds.

Step 2: Make all the muscles in your body go loose and floppy like a ragdoll. Keep your body loose and floppy like a ragdoll for five seconds.

Step 3: Do the Robot-Ragdoll again, but this time, notice how your body feels tight when you are a robot and relaxed when you are a ragdoll. You have the power to make your body relax!

Dear Caregiver,

Today I started reading *Cory's Story* to your child. *Cory's Story* will help your child cope with the death. I will read a chapter of *Cory's Story* to your child over the next few sessions. Each chapter highlights a different issue.

The focus of the first chapter is on introducing Cory to your child. Your child will identify with Cory and realize that they are not the only one dealing with grief. Although the issue of the death is introduced in this chapter, it is not the focus. Children need to ease into talking about difficult issues. This chapter helps to build a positive relationship so your child will feel more comfortable coming to sessions and being open and expressive.

People of different religions, ethnicities, and cultures have different beliefs about death and ways of mourning. I am eager to learn from you the traditions of your culture, religion, and family, and I will be respectful of these throughout our time together. I will modify *Cory's Story* and the activities so they adhere to your customs and beliefs. Please do not hesitate to give me feedback at any time.

Bringing your child to sessions is an important step in helping them cope with the death. Below are some ways **you can help** make sessions more beneficial for your child:

- Tell your child that this is a place where they can talk about their feelings. Let your child know that they can talk about anything in here, and they will not get in trouble for anything they say.

- Bring your child to sessions as scheduled and on time—children do better when they have consistent appointments.

- Keep me informed of significant updates on your child and family so I can plan accordingly. It is best to contact me when your child is not present so concerns can be discussed freely. Whenever possible, please contact me well in advance of the session, rather than at the time of the appointment, so I can plan for the session and so your child can benefit from the full session time.

Your active involvement in sessions is critical to your child's progress. While I will raise issues in our sessions that are focused on helping you support your child, if there are other things you want to talk with me about, please let me know. You have a say in what our plan will be for our sessions, and we will talk more about your ideas and goals.

In today's session, your child learned a relaxation technique called Robot-Ragdoll. Regularly practicing Robot-Ragdoll with your child is an important part of helping them learn ways to cope. It is best to do Robot-Ragdoll with your child each night at bedtime. This will help calm your child in preparation for sleep. You can do Robot-Ragdoll along with your child—it will help your child learn the technique and it will reduce your stress level too!

You can help your child by establishing an age-appropriate bedtime routine and integrating Robot-Ragdoll into it. For example: brush teeth, put on pajamas, read a bedtime story while cuddling together, do Robot-Ragdoll three times, and give hugs and kisses goodnight. Some children will need additional measures to help them feel safe at bedtime (e.g., leaving on a nightlight and sleeping with a comfort object).

Once your child has learned Robot-Ragdoll, you can help them do it when they need to feel calm. You can follow this three-step process:

1. Pay attention to the signs that your child is getting overly upset and name what you see: "You're holding on to me very tightly and you have a scared look on your face."
2. Coach your child to use Robot-Ragdoll to feel calm (do Robot-Ragdoll too so your child can follow your lead): "Let's do Robot-Ragdoll together to feel calm. We'll do it a few times until our bodies relax."
3. Praise your child: "You just did a great job doing Robot-Ragdoll to calm your body."

Attached is a copy of the chapter from today's session so you can better understand what was covered.

Chapter Overview
Learning about Death

Goals
- Verbalize an understanding of death and key concepts related to death and grief
- Identify common feelings and reactions associated with grief
- Increase ability to talk openly about the death

Materials
- Child's scrapbook
- Markers or colored pencils
- Paper
- Questions for the Crumpled Paper Throw Game (included)
- Two copies of "Learning about Death" (one copy for the child's scrapbook, one copy for the caregiver)
- Letter for the caregiver

Guidelines and Process Issues

Death is difficult to talk about and hard to explain to children. It is especially tough to talk with children about "stigmatized" deaths such as suicide, murder, or substance-related deaths. Caregivers may be reluctant to tell the child the truth about how the person died. They may believe that sharing details will harm their child, or their own grief reactions, such as avoidance, may lead to reluctance to talk openly about the death. Convey understanding and empathy for the caregiver's perspective while helping them to understand and accept that children need honest, developmentally comprehensible information about the circumstances of the death.

While it is not helpful for the child to be lied to regarding the cause of death, it is also important not to provide details that are too overwhelming for the child's developmental or cognitive capacities. For example, it is usually not helpful to tell children details that are gruesome, that the person suffered, or that helpers did not do all they could to save the person (Cohen et al., 2017).

Two versions of the caregiver letter are included in this chapter: one for families in which the child knows the general circumstances regarding the death and a second version for families who have not explained how the person died. This second version helps caregivers understand the rationale for talking openly and honestly about the death and offers tips on what to say. Sample explanations are provided in the letter to the caregiver so they are better equipped to explain the cause of death to the child. It might be helpful to role-play with the caregiver so they feel more confident about exactly what to say, before their talk with their child. It may also be helpful to offer to be present when the caregiver has the talk with their child to provide added guidance and support. In this case, meet with the caregiver to prepare before the joint session with their child.

In cases of unconfirmed death, for example, when a body has not been recovered, it is even more confusing and difficult for the child to accept the reality of the death. This can lead to feelings of ambiguous loss. The caregiver may need guidance on helping the child deal with the complex emotions that arise when the death is suspected but not confirmed. A parent information sheet about Unconfirmed Death is available from the National Child Traumatic Stress Network.

The Crumpled Paper Throw Game explains death and related concepts, dispels myths, normalizes common feelings and reactions, provides reassurance, offers coping strategies, and facilitates open communication.

This chapter of Cory's Story and the Crumpled Paper Throw Game should be used with the child only after they have learned the truth from their caregiver regarding how the person died. The story and game can then help children integrate the information and process their feelings and reactions.

During the Crumpled Paper Throw Game, show photos to the child to augment their understanding of some of the terms and concepts. The photos should correspond to the game questions and be relevant to the child's situation, such as a casket, a cemetery, a headstone, burial, an urn, and ashes. These photos can be found online.

Multiple sets of questions are included in the Crumpled Paper Throw Game. **Review the questions before the session and modify as needed to suit the child's circumstances and level of understanding. Remove questions that are inappropriate to the child's situation. Additional questions relevant to the child's circumstances can be added to the game.**

The child might be too young to understand many of the concepts in the Crumpled Paper Throw Game. It can still be useful to introduce the concepts to plant the seed and model direct discussion about death. The game can go into the child's scrapbook as well (which they can take home at the end of their last session) and revisited in later years, when they are better able to grasp the content.

Movement exercises are incorporated into the Crumpled Paper Throw Game to add to the appeal of the activity and to channel energy into a positive outlet. Participate in these exercises along with the child to model and to set a playful tone. (The caregiver can also participate in the movement exercises if they are participating in the session.)

When playing the game, the child stands behind a designated throw line. Stand far enough from the child to make the game challenging but close enough to ensure the child has some success in throwing the crumpled paper through the hoop.

Before the session, it is imperative to meet with the caregiver to review the questions from the Crumpled Paper Throw Game and to modify if needed. It is particularly important to respect the family's cultural and religious beliefs and mourning practices. Ideally, the caregiver should participate in the session and play the game along with the child.

Learning about Death

(**Important note:** The child must be told the truth about the circumstances of the death before reading this chapter of *Cory's Story*. See the Chapter Overview and Letter to the Caregiver for further information.)

Welcome back to the story! Today we're going to learn some important things. We're going to learn what it means to be alive and what it means to be dead. All people are born, they live, and eventually they die. Death happens when a person's body becomes so old, sick, or injured that it stops working and will never work again. When a person dies, their heart stops beating and they stop breathing. A dead body cannot move, play, eat, or sleep. When a person dies, their body does not feel emotions like happy, sad, or scared, and their body cannot feel hurt or pain because their body doesn't work anymore.

When a person dies, their heart stops beating and they stop breathing. You are alive, which means your heart is beating and you are breathing. Jump up and down 20 times, then put your hand on your chest to feel your heart beating and your body breathing.

Dead people don't feel hurt or pain because their bodies don't work anymore. You are alive, which means your body can feel hurt and pain. Pinch your arm (not too hard!).

Dead people don't need to eat because their bodies don't work anymore. You are alive, which means you need to eat. Pretend you are eating your favorite food.

Now Cory understood what it means to be alive and what it means to be dead. But Cory was still confused. Cory asked Ana, "Where do dead people go? Will they come back? Can I do things with them again?" Ana said, "These are all good questions. We're going to play a game to help you learn more about what happens when someone dies. It's called Crumpled Paper Throw." Cory was excited to play the game!

We're going to play the game too. Let's follow the instructions.

Crumpled Paper Throw Game

Crumple a piece of paper into a ball. Stand behind the line, and throw the paper ball toward the hoop I make with my arms. If you get the crumpled paper through the hoop, you get a high-five! If you miss, I will ask you a question. (The questions will help you learn about death.) If you don't get the answer to the question the first time, don't worry—the whole point of the game is to learn about death, so that's why I'll read the answer to the question, and then you can say what you learned. Let's play!

Questions:
Crumpled Paper Throw Game

(Modify or omit questions to suit the child's circumstances and level of understanding. This game may take more than one session, especially for younger children with a limited attention span.)

What does dead mean? Dead is when a person dies. Death happens when a person's body becomes so old, sick, or injured that it stops working and will never work again.

When a person dies, can their body still breathe or move or feel emotions? When a person dies, their body cannot breathe, move, play, eat, or sleep. They do not feel emotions like happy, sad, or scared, and they cannot feel hurt or pain because their body doesn't work anymore.

Can a dead person come back alive? A dead person cannot come back alive, even if we wish really hard. When a body dies, it stops working forever, and so the person who died cannot ever come back alive. You won't see (the deceased) alive again but you can look at photos and talk about (the deceased) and dream about them.

When a person dies, does that mean we cannot do things with them ever again? A dead person cannot come back alive, so when someone dies, we cannot do things with them ever again. (What's something you will miss doing with the person who died?)

Is it normal to wish that the dead person will come back alive? It is normal to wish that the person who died will come back. Even if we wish really hard, the person who died cannot come back alive. It's normal and okay to feel sad that the person who died cannot come back alive.

What is a casket? (Include this question only if the person who died was buried.) A casket is a special box that holds the body of the person who died. Let's look online to find a photo of a casket.

What is a viewing/visitation? After a person dies, there may be a viewing/visitation where we can see the body of the person who died one last time. The body of the person who died may be lying in the casket. It may look like they are sleeping because their eyes are closed and they are not moving. But their eyes are closed and they are not moving because they are dead. Family and friends come to the viewing/visitation and talk to the family of the person who died. They may say nice things to try to help the family feel better. Some children go to the viewing/visitation, and some children don't go.

What is a funeral/memorial service/cremation ceremony? A funeral/memorial service/cremation ceremony is the time when family and friends come to remember the person who died. People tell stories and say nice things about the person who died. Some children go to the funeral/memorial service/cremation ceremony, and some children don't go.

What is a cemetery? (Include this question only if the person who died was buried.) A cemetery is a place where people who have died are buried. At the cemetery, there are headstones that families have put there to show who has died and been buried there. Each headstone has the name of the person who died. Let's look online to find a photo of a cemetery and headstones.

Once the person who died is put in the casket, then what happens to the dead person's body? (Include this question only if the person who died was buried.) The casket holding the body of the person who died is taken to the cemetery. At the cemetery, the casket holding the body of the person who died is put into a deep hole in the ground and covered with earth. Although it may seem strange or scary to put the dead body in the deep hole in the ground, it doesn't bother or upset the person, because dead bodies don't feel anything. They do not feel scared, and they do not feel any pain.

What is cremation? (Include this question only if the person who died was cremated.) Cremation means the dead body is put into a machine that is very hot and this machine turns the dead body into ashes. Ashes look like sand. Being cremated may seem weird, scary, or gross, but the person who died cannot feel anything. It doesn't hurt because dead bodies don't feel pain. Let's look online to find a photo of ashes.

What is an urn? (Include this question only if the person who died was cremated.) After the dead body is cremated and turned into ashes, the ashes are put into a box called an urn. The urn is buried in the ground or put in a building called a mausoleum or kept at home. Some people scatter the ashes in a special place. Let's look online to find a photo of an urn.

Where do dead people go? (Replace with an alternative explanation to suit the family's beliefs.) Some people believe the person's soul leaves the body and goes to heaven. We don't know exactly what happens in heaven but we believe that it is a good place where nothing bad or sad or scary happens. (What do you think happens after a person dies?)

Can you visit the person who died in heaven? (Remove or replace with an alternative explanation to suit the family's beliefs.) You cannot visit the person who died in heaven. But you can imagine what heaven is like.

Is it normal to have a lot of mixed-up feelings when someone dies? Children usually have a lot of mixed-up feelings when someone dies. These mixed-up feelings are called grief. You might feel sad or you might not feel sad. You might feel sad sometimes, and at other times you might feel happy. You might feel guilty or bad about the times when you feel happy. You might have lots of other feelings. Whatever you are feeling is normal and okay. It's okay to have fun, laugh, and play even when something really sad has happened. (What feelings have you had since the person died?)

If you don't cry about the death, does this mean you didn't care about the person who died? Sometimes, people who cared a lot about the person who died don't show their emotions or they don't cry about the death. There is no right or wrong way to feel or react when someone important to you dies.

What if you feel angry or upset with the person who died, or remember things about them that you didn't like? No one is perfect. It is normal and okay to have different feelings about a person who died. It is even normal and okay to be upset with the person because they died. Coming here will help you talk about your feelings.

What are some ways children might react after someone dies? Children usually have upset reactions when someone dies. Some children feel really scared and want to stay close to their parent or safe adult. Some children feel so angry that they have a lot of temper tantrums, or they get stomach aches, have bad dreams, or wet their bed. Coming here will help you learn ways to feel better.

What are some worries children may have after someone dies? Children may worry that more bad things will happen, or that someone else will die. Or they may worry about who will take care of them. Or they may have other worries. This is a place where you can talk about your worries and learn ways to handle them.

What does guilty mean, and is it normal to feel guilty when someone dies? *Guilty* means feeling bad about something we think we did wrong. Some children feel bad that they didn't treat the person better while they were alive, or they think they did something wrong or bad to make the person die, or they think they should have stopped the person from dying. It's important for you to know that nothing you said or did made the person die and you cannot do anything to make the dead person come back alive.

Is it normal and okay to feel relieved after someone dies? People sometimes feel relieved or even happy when the person dies. If the person was very sick or in a lot of pain, then they might feel relieved that the person is no longer in pain. Some people didn't get along well with the person and are glad the person is gone. Some people have mixed-up feelings of happy and sad when the person dies. Whatever you are feeling is okay.

Is it best to pretend to be happy so you don't make your (caregiver) more upset? Many children think that they should pretend to be happy so they don't make their (caregiver) more upset. But it's okay to feel your feelings, show your feelings, and talk about your feelings. You don't need to worry about hiding your true feelings from your (caregiver), because grown-ups can take care of themselves.

If someone asks you about the death and you don't want to talk about it, what can you do? It's okay to say "I don't feel like talking about that right now." You get to decide when you talk about it and when you don't.

If you have questions about the person who died or about the death, what can you do? Talk to your (caregiver) or to another caring adult. They may not be able to answer all your questions, but they will try. You may think your (caregiver) doesn't want to talk about the death, but that's not true. Your (caregiver) wants you to talk to them, even about things that are really hard. (What questions do you have about the person who died or about the death?)

Additional Questions:
Crumpled Paper Throw Game
(Version for Cancer. Modify for other illnesses.)

(Modify or omit questions to suit the child's circumstances and level of understanding.)

What is cancer? Cancer is when sick cells grow in the body. These sick cells make it hard for the body to work properly.

Why do some people get cancer? Nobody knows why some people get cancer. Even the best, smartest doctors in the whole world do not know why some people get cancer.

Can a child's misbehavior make someone get cancer? Nothing a child does or says can make someone get cancer. People's words, thoughts, or misbehavior never make someone get cancer. We don't know why someone gets cancer. But we know for sure that our words, thoughts, or misbehavior never make someone get cancer.

How do doctors try to help someone who has cancer? Doctors try to help someone who has cancer in different ways. For example, they might do surgery (a special operation where they try to remove the parts of the body that have cancer). They might give the person chemotherapy (also called chemo), which is a medicine that works hard to get rid of the cancer. Radiation is another cancer treatment doctors may use to try to get rid of cancer. Doctors try their very best to make the cancer go away, but sadly, sometimes the person does not get better and they die.

What are the side effects of cancer treatments? People who get cancer treatments or cancer medicine may feel very tired. They may feel sick and even throw up. Their hair may fall out and they get a bald head. It can be confusing and scary for kids when this happens. (What do you remember happening to the person who died when they were sick from cancer, and how did it make you feel?)

If someone in your family died from cancer, can you get cancer from that person and die too? You cannot get cancer from someone like you can get a cold from someone. A cold is an illness that is contagious. If someone has a cold, and that person coughs or sneezes near you, you may get the cold from the person who has the cold. Cancer is an illness that is NOT contagious. That means that you or others in your family cannot get sick from cancer from the person who had it.

If someone in your family gets sick, will they die too? Everyone gets sick sometimes. Most people who get sick get better with rest and medicine. (Tell about a time you got sick and what helped you to get better.)

Additional Questions:
Crumpled Paper Throw Game
(Version for Suicide)

(Modify or omit questions to suit the child's circumstances and level of understanding.)

What is suicide? Suicide is when someone makes their own body stop working so that they die.

After a suicide, how come some parents may not tell their children what really happened? Parents may not tell their children at first about the suicide because they worry that their children will feel very upset and confused. Instead of saying the person died by suicide, they may say that the person died another way like from a heart attack or from a bad accident. But with help, parents learn ways to talk to their children about suicide and to help them with any feelings they have about it.

Why would someone die by suicide? We don't know the exact reason why. They may have mistakenly believed that their problems were so hard that the only way to get away from these problems is to stop living. We know this isn't true, but the person who died by suicide probably felt like this was true for them in that moment. When someone dies by suicide, it doesn't make them a bad person; it just means their body had an illness that made their brain not think clearly.

(Alternative explanation) Why would someone die by suicide? We don't know the exact reason why. They may have felt a kind of sadness that is much sadder than regular sadness (called depression) and their brain was not able to think properly. Some people believe that the only way to solve their very sad feelings is to make their own body stop working. Their very sad feelings can often make it hard to remember other ways to get better. When someone dies by suicide, it doesn't make them a bad person; it just means their body had an illness that made their brain not think clearly.

Why do some people feel angry when someone dies by suicide? People may feel angry when someone dies by suicide. They may feel angry at the person for dying by suicide or at themselves for not stopping the person from dying by suicide. Coming here will help you talk about your feelings and learn ways to feel better.

Why do some children feel guilty or bad when someone dies by suicide? Children may feel like their misbehavior made the person die by suicide. All children misbehave sometimes. Nothing you said or did made the person die by suicide.

Why do some children believe that the person who died by suicide did not love them or care about them? Some children may think that the person who died by suicide did not love them or care about them. But when someone dies by suicide, their brain is not thinking right, so they may have a hard time feeling happy for all the wonderful things around them, like you!

Why do some kids feel confused or mixed-up about suicide? Suicide is hard to understand, so it's normal to feel confused or mixed-up. If you feel confused or mixed up about the suicide, talk to your (caregiver) or to another caring adult. They will do their best to answer your questions. (What questions do you have about the suicide?)

Additional Questions:
Crumpled Paper Throw Game
(Version for Murder, Mass Violence, Hate-Based Violence)

(Modify or omit questions to suit the child's circumstances and level of understanding.)

What is murder? Murder means someone kills another person on purpose. They hurt the person's body so badly that they make the person's body stop working forever. When murder (or killing) happens, it can feel very sad and scary and hard to understand why it happened. Coming here will help you with your mixed-up feelings.

What is mass violence? Mass violence happens when several people are injured or killed by someone. When this happens, it can feel very sad and scary and hard to understand why it happened. Coming here will help you with your mixed-up feelings.

What is hate-based violence? Some people hurt or kill others because of the color of their skin, their religion, or their gender identity. When this happens, it can feel very sad and scary and hard to understand why it happened. It is wrong to treat other people so badly. Coming here will help you with your mixed-up feelings.

How come some parents may not tell their children what really happened? Parents may not tell their kids at first about the murder (shooting, attack) because they worry that their children will feel very upset and confused. Instead of telling them what really happened, they may say that the person died another way like in a bad accident. But with help, parents learn ways to talk to their children about what really happened and to help them with any feelings they have about it.

Why would someone murder or kill another person? It's hard to understand why someone would murder or kill another person because it is so awful and wrong. Sometimes the person who did it explains why they did it, but no matter what happened, murder is always wrong. Sometimes we never find out what really happened, and that can be even more confusing and upsetting.

If the person who did the killing or the murder is someone in your family, is it okay to still love that person? It is normal to have lots of mixed-up feelings toward the person who did the killing or the murder. You may be angry at the person for doing it. You may be scared of the person who did it. You may still love the person even though they did something so awful. You may have all these feelings at the same time. (How do you feel toward the person who did the killing or the murder?)

Why do some children feel guilty or bad when someone is murdered? Children may feel like their misbehavior made the person die. But the only one to blame for the murder is the person who did it. Nothing you said or did made it happen.

Why do some people feel angry when someone is murdered? Anger is a common feeling to have when someone is murdered. People may feel angry at the person who did it, at the person who was killed for not getting away, or at themselves for not stopping it. They may want to hurt the person who did it. It is normal and okay to feel angry, but it is important to let out anger in ways that don't hurt you or others.

Why do some children feel more worried and afraid when someone is murdered? It is normal to feel worried and afraid because something very bad and scary happened. Children may have scary thoughts or bad dreams about it. They may worry that other bad things will happen. They may feel afraid to be alone or to go certain places. There are things children can do to feel safer, like thinking of a happy place, sleeping with a stuffed animal or nightlight, staying close to a safe adult, and telling themselves that they are safe now.

Who are first responders? First responders are the people who come to help when someone has been badly hurt. Doctors, nurses and ambulance workers help people who are hurt. Firefighters, police officers, and other people also come to help.

Why do some children feel scared to go back to the place where the murder (shooting, attack) happened? It's normal to feel scared to go back to the place (home, school, neighborhood) where something so terrible happened. When you feel scared, look for the grown-up helpers and this will help you feel better. Special helpers have made your (school, neighborhood) a safer place by (add ideas such as putting locks on the door, adding more police). (What are your ideas for feeling safer?)

How come the death is on the TV/news/internet? When something very sad like a murder happens, it might be on the TV/news/internet so that others can learn what happened, and sometimes, help if they can. There may be people with cameras trying to take pictures of your family. This can seem weird or even scary. (How do you feel about the death being on the TV/news/internet?)

Additional Questions:
Crumpled Paper Throw Game
(Version for Military Casualties)

(Modify or omit questions to suit the child's circumstances and level of understanding.)

How are families usually told that the person died? Usually, people from the military come to the family's home to tell them the very sad news that the person died. There may not be a lot of information about how and where the person died. This can make it even harder and more confusing. Sometimes, the family hears something about the death on the news or on social media. (How did you find out that the person died? Who told you and what did they say?)

What are accidental or friendly fire deaths? Sometimes, the person dies by accident, like when they are training to do their job, or someone kills them by mistake. When this happens, it can be very upsetting and confusing.

What are some of the things that happen at a military funeral? Every funeral is different, but these are some things that may happen at a military funeral: The country's flag is draped over the casket and later it gets folded and given to the family; a special song called Taps is played; people called honor guards may fire their rifles. Some children may feel confused or scared by what happens at the funeral. It's okay to ask questions and talk to your (caregiver) or another caring adult about your feelings. (If you went to the funeral, what do you remember about it? What feelings did you have at the funeral?)

How might a child feel if (the deceased) was away for a long time before they died? People who are in the military are often away from their families for a long time. This is called deployment. Children may think the person will come back, like they did before, but, unfortunately, the person has died and can never come back. Children usually have a lot of mixed-up feelings when the person dies. Whatever you are feeling is normal and okay.

What does the ultimate sacrifice mean? When people say your (deceased) made the ultimate sacrifice or was a fallen hero, they mean the person died trying to make our world a better place.

Why do some people feel angry when their family member is killed in the line of duty? Anger is a common feeling to have when someone is killed in the line of duty. People may feel angry at the person responsible for killing them or at the person who was killed for choosing to be in the military or for not getting away. It's normal and okay to feel angry, but it's important to let out anger in ways that don't hurt you or others.

Is it normal to have mixed-up feelings that your family member chose to serve in the military? It's normal to have good and upset feelings about this. You may have good feelings because you are proud that they chose to serve and protect the country. You may also be upset that because they chose to serve in the military, they are now dead. Whatever you are feeling is normal and okay. (How do you feel about your family member serving in the military?)

What does *guilty* mean, and is it normal to feel guilty when a family member is killed in the line of duty? Guilty means feeling bad about something we think we did wrong. Children may feel guilty or bad for not spending more time with their family member when they were home, for not treating the person better when they were alive, or for not being better behaved. They may think their bad behavior made the person die. It's important for you to know that nothing you said or did made the person die.

What is *relocation*? Relocation means the family has to move. It can be hard to move to a new home and to change schools. It can be hard to leave friends and to make new friends. (How do you feel about the move or the relocation? What has been hard for you about the move or the relocation? What changes have you liked since the move or the relocation?)

Additional Questions:
Crumpled Paper Throw Game
(Version for Substance-Related Death)

(Modify or omit questions to suit the child's circumstances and level of understanding.)

What are drugs? Lots of people take medicine (also called drugs) when they are sick. Medicine or drugs are given by doctors to help people get better when they are sick. Doctors are careful about how much medicine or drugs to give people to stay safe, and it's important to follow the doctor's instructions. Some people take too many drugs (or illegal drugs, like heroin or meth) because they like the feeling it causes, even though it is very bad for their bodies or brains. Then, because of what those drugs do to their brains, they can't stop taking them even when bad things happen.

If people get sick and take medicine (drugs), will they die too? Medicine is almost always safe when someone takes the amount the doctor says.

What is drug addiction/substance use disorder (SUD)? It is a disease that affects the brain. It can happen when someone drinks alcohol too much or takes a lot of drugs. This disease fools the brain into thinking that the body needs drugs/alcohol to survive. Then they can't stop using drugs even when bad things happen and they could die.

Why would someone use drugs if they know they can be harmful? Some people like the way drugs make them feel. Drugs change the way a person's brain works. Then people find it really hard to stop taking drugs.

What does getting high mean? Getting high means using a lot of drugs. When someone gets high, they can't think properly. They may act weird, or they may even become mean or scary.

How might kids feel when someone in their family has a substance use disorder? If someone in a family has a substance use disorder, things at home might not feel calm or safe. Kids may feel worried, scared, angry, sad, embarrassed, guilty, confused, or other feelings. Coming here will help you talk about your feelings and learn ways to feel better.

Why do families sometimes want the substance use disorder to be a secret? People may not want to tell others about their substance use disorder. They may worry that others will think badly of them. Sometimes kids think that if they talk about a parent's drug use, they will get their parent in trouble or they will get in trouble themselves. This is a place where you can talk about anything.

What can help a person who has a substance use disorder? A substance use disorder can be treated. With help and support, many people can stop using substances that are dangerous for them. This is called recovery. There are different recovery plans to help people with a substance use disorder. Recovery is a decision the person has to make for themselves. No one else can make the decision for them. So there is nothing you did bad to make the person get the substance use disorder, and it's not up to you to make the person better.

What is a substance overdose? An overdose is when someone accidentally or on purpose takes too many drugs or when there is something in the drug that the person didn't know about. The overdose can make them very sick or it can make their body stop working and the person dies. Children have lots of mixed-up feelings when someone dies from an overdose. Coming here will help you learn ways to feel better.

Additional Questions:
Crumpled Paper Throw Game
(Version for Natural Disaster)

(Modify or omit questions to suit the child's circumstances and level of understanding.)

What are natural disasters? Natural disasters are bad things that happen to the Earth that cause a lot of damage like hurricanes, earthquakes, floods, wildfires, and tsunamis. Sometimes people get badly hurt or die during a natural disaster. Natural disasters are very rare, which means they hardly ever happen. It's normal to have a lot of upset feelings when someone dies in a natural disaster. Coming here will help you learn ways to feel better. (Add additional information that is specific to the type of natural disaster the child experienced.)

Who are first responders? When a (type of natural disaster) happens, many people come to help. Doctors, nurses and ambulance workers help people who are hurt. Firefighters put out the fires. Police officers help keep people safe. Diggers and other workers look for missing people and clean up the damage. Many others come to help.

What are scary reminders and what can kids do about them? Scary reminders are things that remind people of the (type of natural disaster) like loud noises, the sound of sirens, the smell of fire, people running or crying or screaming, or storms. Coming here will help you learn ways to cope with your scared feelings.

What does evacuation mean? In an evacuation, you have to leave your home because it's not safe to stay and you go somewhere that is safe.

Where do people go if their home is damaged? Some people move to a place called a shelter or a settlement camp. It can be hard to move away from home, especially if you don't have the things that are important to you like favorite toys or a stuffed animal. But you are in a safe place now.

Can a child's misbehavior make it happen? Nothing a child does or says makes a (type of natural disaster) happen. Sometimes disasters happen and there is no reason and it's no one's fault. It helps to know that the (type of natural disaster) don't happen often and you are safe right now.

What can kids do if they're worried that the (type of natural disaster) will happen again? What happened was really scary. It's normal to worry that it will happen again. It's important to know that (type of natural disaster) don't happen often and you are safe right now.

Breaks:
Crumpled Paper Throw Game
(Intersperse these throughout the game.)

Take a break to move your body: Stomp your feet five times, then freeze your body for five seconds.

Take a break to move your body: Jog on the spot for five seconds then, freeze your body for five seconds.

Take a break to move your body: Stretch your body by lacing your fingers together and raising your hands above your head, palms facing upward. Hold this pose for five seconds.

Take a break to move your body: Do the shoulder scrunch by scrunching your shoulders up to your ears, then relaxing them and moving them around five times.

Take a break to move your body: Do neck circles by placing your hands on your hips, and circling your head in one direction three times, then in the other direction three times.

Take a break to move your body: Touch your shoulders, then your knees, then your toes, then your nose.

Take a break to move your body: Hop to the other end of the room and back on one foot.

Take a break to move your body: Walk once around the room in slow motion.

Take a break to move your body: Walk once around the room really fast.

Take a break to move your body: Shake hands with the person beside you.

Take a break to move your body: Give a high-five to the person beside you.

(Version for caregivers who have told the child the circumstances of the death)

Dear Caregiver,

Today's chapter focused on explaining death and related concepts. Children often feel scared and confused about these concepts, so the purpose of the session was to explain key issues and alleviate fears.

It can be difficult to talk about death. However, children cope better when their caregivers talk with them about the death in an open and age-appropriate manner. Here are some tips to guide you and to help you prepare for the conversations:

- Show that you are listening by making and keeping eye contact, nodding, and repeating back what your child has said.

- Invite dialogue about any questions or worries your child might have: "It's normal to feel confused or worried. What questions or worries do you have about the death?" Answer questions honestly. Usually, when a child asks a question about what happened, they are ready to hear the answer. If you don't know the answer, say "That's a good question but I don't know. If I find out the answer, I will tell you." The internet is an excellent source of information. Check in with your child periodically to ask about any questions or worries that have come up.

- Your child might ask the same question about the death over and over. This is because they are trying to make sense of difficult information. Even if you have already answered their question, repeat your response calmly and patiently.

- Young children have difficulty understanding the concept of death and its finality. Even if they have been told repeatedly that the person who died will not come back, young children may continue to believe that the person will return. This chapter explains death and its finality. Help your child grasp the concept of death by pointing out things around you that are living and things that are dead. For example, point to an ant that you see on the ground and say "This ant is alive. See, it is moving." Then find an ant that is dead and point out that it is not moving and cannot feel anything. Then relate this to the person who died by saying "The ant is dead and cannot come back alive, just like (the deceased) is dead and cannot come back alive."

- Use accurate words and language. Although it may be difficult to use the words died and dead, it's better than using confusing euphemisms. For example, if you say "he went to sleep," the child might say "so wake him up" or if you say "we've lost him," the child might say "let's go find him."

- Listen to and validate your child's feelings, and invite them to share more: "I know this is very hard. Tell me about your feelings." You can also invite them to draw you a picture of their feelings.

- Don't be afraid to show emotion. If you grieve openly, it gives your child permission to grieve openly. Put words to your emotions and offer reassurance—for example, "I'm crying because I am sad that (____) died. But even though I feel sad, I can still take care of you."

- It is normal for children to think that they somehow caused the death. Alleviate guilt by repeatedly saying "You did not make (____) die, and you cannot bring (____) back alive."

Learning about Death

- Alleviate your child's fear that other family members will die soon too: "Most people live a long and healthy life. I expect to live for a long time."

- If your child witnessed any frightening aspect of the death, initiate age-appropriate discussion that validates their feelings – for example, "It was scary when the car crashed and (the deceased) got badly hurt and died."

- Reassure your child they will be cared for—for example, "There will always be adults to take care of you, like Aunt Lisa."

Attached is a copy of the chapter from today's session so you can better understand what was covered.

(Version for caregivers who have not told the child the actual circumstances of the death)

(**Note:** This is difficult and sensitive information to share with the caregiver and is better delivered in a face-to-face session than in a letter. The letter outlines discussion points to use with the caregiver and can be given to them after the session to reinforce what was said.)

Dear Caregiver,

Death is difficult to talk about and hard to explain to children. In cases like suicide, murder, or substance-related death, there is often a stigma that can make it even harder to talk about. Families often feel ashamed, angry, or confused. These feelings make the grieving process more painful.

You may believe it is best to shield your child from the truth, that somehow this will protect them. But experts believe that the opposite is true. Hiding the truth about how the person died can do more harm than good. Here are some reasons why it's important to be open and honest with children about how the person died:

- Children are sensitive to change and will pick up that something is happening in their family that they don't know about. This makes them anxious.

- If adults avoid open discussion with children, this sends the message that it is not okay to talk about death or what happened. Children might then shut down and keep their thoughts and feelings to themselves.

- When not given all information, children make up stories in their minds, often blaming themselves.

- If children are lied to and later they learn the truth (as almost always happens), it can be difficult to regain their trust. They might think "If you lied to me about this, what else are you lying to me about?"

- It is natural to spare children from the truth by making up another explanation. However, children often find out the truth by overhearing a conversation, seeing it on the news, or hearing about it from someone else. It is better for children to be given accurate information by a caring adult rather than hearing rumors.

- When children hear the truth directly from you first, you can help shape their thinking about it. When children are told the details of the death in a planned and appropriate way, it provides an opportunity to process their feelings, answer their questions, and reassure them that they are safe and will be cared for.

- Talking with children about difficult issues and helping them to process the information equips them to handle tough things in the future. It sends the message that you are a safe person to talk to about difficult topics.

You might feel nervous about having this talk with your child or feel unsure about what to say. I am here to guide and support you. Here are some tips:

- Have this talk when your child is not tired or hungry or upset with you.

- Provide your child with physical comfort while talking with them—for example, gently rub their back.

- Show that you are listening by making and keeping eye contact, nodding, and repeating back what they have said.

Learning about Death

- Begin by asking your child what they already know—for example, "Mommy is not here. What do you think happened to her?"

- If your child wasn't initially told the truth about the cause of death, then begin by saying "I didn't tell you the truth about how (___) died because I didn't know what to say. But I got help, so now I'm ready to tell you what really happened."

- Provide an honest, short, simple explanation of what happened, using words your child will understand. Use direct language (dead, NOT gone, asleep, lost, or passed away).

- While it is not helpful for the child to be lied to regarding the cause of death, it is also important not to provide details that are too overwhelming for younger children to process. For example, it is usually not helpful to tell children details that are gory or graphic, that the person suffered, or that helpers did not do all they could to save the person.

- If your child is old enough to understand more details, ask if they would like to know more and then be guided by their response. You may worry about the detrimental impact of sharing more details. However, it is better for children to hear the information from you in a planned and sensitive manner. If a child says they don't want to hear more just now, tell them that they can always come back to you later for more information.

- Listen to and validate your child's feelings, and invite them to share more: "I know this is very hard. Tell me about your feelings."

- Don't be afraid to show emotion. If you grieve openly, it gives your child permission to grieve openly. Put words to your emotions and offer reassurance—for example, "I'm crying because I am sad that (___) died. But even though I feel sad, I can still take care of you."

- Reassure your child they will be cared for—for example, "There will always be adults to take care of you, like Aunt Lisa"

- It is normal for children to think that they somehow caused the death. Alleviate guilt by repeatedly saying "You did not make (___) die, and you cannot bring (___) back alive."

- Alleviate your child's fear that other family members will die soon too: "Most people live a long and healthy life. I expect to live for a long time."

- Keeping children informed will alleviate their anxiety. Explain the process that will be followed and what will happen next.

- Ask children to summarize what you have said to make sure they have understood.

- Invite dialogue about any questions or worries your child might have: "It's normal to feel confused or worried. What questions or worries do you have?" Answer questions honestly. Usually, when a child asks a question about what happened, they are ready to hear the answer. If you don't know the answer, say "That's a good question but I don't know. If I find out I will tell you." Check in with your child periodically to ask about any questions or worries that have come up.

- Your child might ask the same question about the death over and over. This is because they are trying to make sense of difficult information. Even if you have already answered their question, repeat your response calmly and patiently.

- Young children have difficulty understanding the finality of death. Even if they have been told repeatedly that the person who died will not come back, young children may continue to believe that the person will return. Help your child grasp the concept of death by pointing out things around you that are living and things that are dead. For example, point to an ant that you see on the ground and say "This ant is alive. See, it is moving." Then find an ant that is dead and point out that it is not moving and cannot feel anything. Then relate this to the deceased by saying "The ant is dead and cannot come back alive, just like (the deceased) is dead and cannot come back alive."

- Ensure that all caregivers, significant relatives, teacher, and other caring adults in the child's life use similar language when discussing the death with the child to avoid confusion.

- Plan to have future discussions about the details of the death as children express a readiness to hear more: "Now that you seem ready, I'd like to tell you more about how (___) died."

Below are some sample explanations. Keep in mind that each situation is different. Modify what you say so it is appropriate to your situation and your child's ability to understand. Begin with "I have something very upsetting to tell you..."

Sudden Death

"(___) had a (heart attack, aneurysm). This means (___'s) (heart, brain) stopped working. It couldn't be fixed and (___) died. I wish it weren't true, but I am sad to say that this is how (___) died."

Accident

"A sad thing happened with a (car, motorcycle). (___'s) body was hurt and could not be fixed, and (___) died. I wish it weren't true, but I am sad to say that this is how (___) died."

Illness

"(___) had an illness called (___). The doctors tried but I'm sad to say that they couldn't make (___) better and (___) died."

(Provide additional information related to the illness. Search online for guidance on what to say.)

Murder

"Murder means someone kills another person on purpose. They hurt the person's body so badly that they make the person's body stop working forever. I wish it weren't true, but I am sad to say that this is how (___) died."

If the person who committed the murder has not been identified, say "We don't know who killed (___). The police are looking for clues to try to find the person who did it. It's really hard not knowing who killed (___)."

If your child asks how the person was killed, then they are usually ready to hear more detail, or they may have overheard a conversation and want clarification. Provide an honest answer without sharing gory details—for example, "(___) got into a big fight and was killed by (___) with a (gun, knife)," Or "Someone with a gun shot a lot of people, and (___) was one of the people who was shot and killed."

Learning about Death

Suicide

"(___) died by suicide. This means (___) made their body stop working so that they would die. I wish it weren't true, but I am sad to say that this is how (___) died."

Older children: "(___) died by suicide. They made their body stop working so they would die. When someone dies by suicide, they may have very sad feelings, or their brain was not able to think properly. Some people make the mistake of believing that the only way to solve their very sad feelings is to end their own life. Sometimes people have problems inside their brain that make it hard to remember other ways to get better and use all the help that is available."

If your child asks how they made their body stop working, then they are usually ready to hear more detail, or they may have overheard a conversation and want clarification. Provide an honest answer without sharing gory details—for example, "They hung themselves. This means that they used a rope to stop their breathing."

Accidental Overdose

"(___) died of something called an overdose. (___) didn't mean for it to happen, but (___) took too much (medicine, drugs, alcohol) and it made (___'s) body stop working, so (___) died. I wish it weren't true, but I am sad to say that this is how (___) died."

Military Casualties

"What we think happened is that there was a big explosion and (___) was hurt so badly that (___) died. (___) was a hero because (___) died trying to make our world a better place."

There is no easy way to tell your child something so difficult. Conversations like these will be upsetting, but afterwards you'll feel relieved that you were honest and able to build a foundation of trust.

Chapter Overview
Feelings

Goals
- Verbally articulate a range of feelings
- Tolerate (rather than avoid or deny) upsetting emotions

Materials
- Child's scrapbook
- Markers or colored pencils
- Feeling Word Squares (included)
- Scissors
- Two copies of "Feelings" (one copy for the child's scrapbook, one copy for the caregiver)
- Letter for the caregiver

Guidelines and Process Issues

Affective expression and modulation help children openly express and manage feelings more effectively. Bereaved children might detach from their emotions. They might experience feelings they don't have words for or don't know how to articulate. To regulate emotions, children must develop awareness and understanding of internal states and be able to openly express their feelings.

Guess Which Hand is a game to help children expand their emotional vocabulary and identify feeling states. The game begins by helping children verbally express primary emotions (happy, sad, angry, and scared). Grief can lead to a wide range of other emotions. Accordingly, the game helps children expand their emotional vocabulary beyond the primary emotions.

During the game, if the child is having difficulty verbalizing their feelings, then provide examples they can relate to (e.g., Brave is doing something that's scary to do, like jumping into the deep end of the swimming pool for the first time). As the child talks about their feelings, it is helpful to make reflective comments, ask them to elaborate, and validate how they feel.

The Feeling Words for the game have been specifically ordered so that primary emotions (happy, sad, angry, scared) are chosen first. Children with a limited attention span might only be able to manage a few rounds of the game. Use discretion to determine how many rounds to play and which emotions to select. Additional rounds can be played in subsequent sessions.

Emotion coaching is one of the goals of the caregiver session. Initially, this involves teaching the caregiver how to label the child's emotions and providing them with tips on how to facilitate open communication between themselves and their child.

The caregiver is taught the Pillow Talk technique. The goal of this intervention is to open communication between the child and their caregiver and help the caregiver learn and use active listening skills. Pillow Talk is best taught through a combination of verbal discussion and role-plays in the caregiver session, followed by coaching in the conjoint session. Encourage the caregiver to implement Pillow Talk on a nightly basis.

Feelings

Welcome back to the story! Today we're going to talk about feelings. Ana explained, "Everyone has feelings. Sometimes we feel happy, like when we get a present. Sometimes we feel sad, like when a friend moves far away. Sometimes we feel angry, like when we don't get what we want. And sometimes we feel scared, like when we have a bad dream. Everyone has feelings. Happy, sad, angry, and scared are some of the ways we sometimes feel. We're going to play a game today to help us talk about feelings. It's called Guess Which Hand. Let's follow the instructions to learn how to play." Cory was excited to play the game!

We're going to play the game too! Let's follow the instructions:

Guess Which Hand

This is a fun game to help us talk about feelings. I'm going to pick a Feeling Square (e.g., happy), cut it out, fold it several times, and place it in one hand. I will put my hands behind my back and move the folded Feeling Square from hand to hand a few times. Then you will try to guess which hand is holding the Feeling Square. If you guess the hand that's holding the feeling square, you get a high-five! Then we will take turns telling a time we experienced the feeling. If you don't guess the hand that's holding the Feeling Square, then we will start again until you guess the hand that's holding the Feeling Square. I will write your answers below:

I feel happy when: _____

I feel sad when: _____

I feel angry when: _____

I feel scared when: _____

I feel guilty when: _____

I feel jealous when: _____

I feel frustrated when: _____

I feel disappointed when: _____

I feel worried when: _____

I feel shocked when: _____

I feel brave when: _____

I feel yucky when: _____

I feel confused when: _____

I feel proud when: _____

I feel loved when: _____

Guess Which Hand Game:
Feeling Squares

HAPPY Something good happens	**SAD** Something upsets you	**ANGRY** You don't like what happened
SCARED Something scary or dangerous is happening	**GUILTY** You know you did something wrong	**JEALOUS** Someone has something you want
FRUSTRATED You try to do something but you can't do it	**DISAPPOINTED** You want something to happen and it doesn't	**WORRIED** You think something bad is going to happen
SHOCKED You can't believe something happened	**BRAVE** You do something that's very scary	**YUCKY** You think something is disgusting
CONFUSED You don't know the answer to something	**PROUD** You do something well	**LOVED** Someone cares about you a lot

Dear Caregiver,

It is important for children to develop a feelings vocabulary and to learn appropriate ways to express their emotions. **You can help** your child by modeling the open expression of feelings. If you express your emotions in an open and appropriate way, it will help your child express emotions in an appropriate way! Here are some specific ideas to help your child express emotions in a healthy way:

- Label your own emotions to help your child learn a Feelings Vocabulary. For example, "I feel frustrated because I am trying to open this jar and I can't" or "I feel proud of myself for baking this beautiful cake."
- Explore your child's feelings and invite open discussion. For example, "What are you feeling right now?" (For a younger child, offer options to choose from such as "Are you feeling sad, angry, or another feeling?") "Tell me more about why you're feeling ___."
- Make talk time part of your nightly routine. Do Pillow Talk each night at bedtime: Sit or lie beside your child in bed, and ask "How was your day today? Was it a happy day or a sad day, or a happy and sad day? What happened to make it a happy day or a sad day?" If your child talks about something upsetting that happened, validate their feelings—for example, "It's upsetting when other kids are mean to you." Don't feel like you must make it all better—simply listening to your child and validating their feelings is what your child needs most from you. And try to do Pillow Talk every night at bedtime. If your child seems reluctant to talk openly with you, don't force the issue—sometimes children need time to open up.

Attached is a copy of the chapter from today's session so you can better understand what was covered.

Chapter Overview
Feelings and Reactions about the Death

(**Important note:** In cases of traumatic grief, move this chapter after the trauma narration component. Children should tell their trauma story before identifying, expressing, and processing their feelings related to the death.)

Goals
- Describe feelings related to the death
- Tolerate (rather than avoid or deny) upsetting emotions
- Implement adaptive coping strategies

Materials
- Child's scrapbook
- Markers or colored pencils
- Two copies of "Feelings and Reactions about the Death" (one copy for the child's scrapbook, one copy for the caregiver)
- Letter for the caregiver

Guidelines and Process Issues

Children often feel overwhelmed by their grief and experience a mix of emotions and reactions. It is important to help children identify, describe, and express feeling states that are commonly associated with bereavement. Children will identify with many of the feelings expressed by Cory in this chapter. This can help reduce children's sense of isolation as they realize that other children have experienced similar feelings and reactions.

While the story normalizes feelings and reactions and facilitates open communication, some children remain guarded, especially about painful emotions. Strategies to encourage openness include asking children to say which of Cory's feelings and reactions they identify with the most or which feelings they think were the hardest for Cory to talk about.

This session encourages the use of a coping strategy called Stop! Freeze! Cookie Breathe! This technique will be most effective if taught to both the child and their caregiver, practiced daily at bedtime, and modeled by the caregiver. Once the child has mastered this technique in calm settings, they can be coached by their caregiver to use it when they need to self-regulate. This technique alone will not be enough to help children to manage strong emotions. It is beyond the scope of this book to detail a comprehensive emotional regulation protocol; therefore, additional interventions to support children and their caregivers should be explored.

The caregiver letter reviews common emotions experienced by grieving children. Emotional support skills are reviewed and tips for reassuring the child are provided.

Caregivers are taught a technique called the Brag Book. When used consistently, the Brag Book increases the child's desirable behavior, elevates their self-esteem, and improves the parent-child relationship.

Feelings and Reactions about the Death

Welcome back to the story! Today we're going to talk more about feelings. When someone dies, we have many different feelings about what happened. It is okay to feel however you feel about the death. Ana asked Cory, "What are some of the feelings you have had since (the deceased) died?" Cory said, "I don't want to talk about my feelings. I just want to pretend that everything is fine." Ana replied, "It can be hard to talk about feelings. Many children want to pretend that everything is fine. But talking about your feelings is a good way to help yourself feel better." Cory wanted to feel better, so Cory talked to Ana.

Cory told Ana, "Sometimes I feel happy like when I'm playing or doing something fun. Sometimes I feel sad because I miss (the deceased). Sometimes I cry. Sometimes (the caregiver) cries. I don't like it when (the caregiver) cries." Ana said, "Cory, it's okay to feel happy and it's okay to feel sad. When you feel sad, it's okay to cry. And it's okay for your (the caregiver) to cry. Sad feelings don't stay forever."

What makes Cory feel happy?

What makes you feel happy?

Show with your face and body what happy looks like.

Does Cory feel sad sometimes?

Is it okay to cry if you feel sad?

Show with your face and body what sad looks like.

What makes you feel sad?

Do sad feelings stay forever?

Ana said, "Cory, you did a good job showing with your face and body what happy and sad looks like! Tell me more about your feelings." Cory said, "Sometimes I feel angry. It's no fair I don't have my (the deceased) anymore. It's no fair I can't do things with (the deceased) anymore. Everything's different now and I don't like it. I'm angry!"

What makes Cory feel angry?

What makes you feel angry?

When Cory feels angry, Cory's face gets an angry look. When Cory feels very, very angry, Cory sometimes throws a tantrum. This is when Cory yells and hits and kicks! Ana explained, "Cory, it's okay to feel angry, but it's not okay to yell or hit or kick. When you feel angry, you can get calm by doing Stop! Freeze! Cookie Breathe!" Ana taught Cory how to do it.

Let's learn Stop! Freeze! Cookie Breathe! and then do it together:

1. Say to yourself: "Stop!"
2. Freeze your body (don't move your body) for three seconds.
3. Picture in your mind your favorite kind of cookie.
4. Do Cookie Breathing to calm your body. (To do Cookie Breathing, imagine your favorite kind of cookie freshly baked, hot out of the oven. Smell the yummy cookies and then blow on them to cool them down. When you smell the cookies, breathe in through your nose for three seconds, then blow out through your mouth for four seconds. Do this three times or until your body is calm.)

Cory said, "Hey, it worked—I got calm by doing Stop! Freeze! Cookie Breathe! I feel better!" Ana was proud of Cory for doing such a good job doing Stop! Freeze! Cookie Breathe! Ana asked Cory, "Tell me more about your feelings." Cory got an upset look. Cory said, "I feel like I'm bad. Sometimes I don't listen. Sometimes I do bad things. Then I get in trouble and I feel more bad." Ana reassured Cory, "All kids misbehave sometimes. No child acts perfectly good all the time." Cory interrupted Ana and said, "But I'm bad. I made my (the deceased) get dead because when we had a fight, I said I hated them and wished they were dead. So I made it happen ... I made them get dead!" Ana replied, "people's words or thoughts never make someone die. Nothing you said or did made your (the deceased) die. It is very sad that your (the deceased) died. But you did not make your (the deceased) die." Cory felt better hearing this.

Do children act perfectly all the time?

If Cory misbehaves, does this mean Cory is bad?

If you misbehave, does this mean you are bad?

Can people's words or thoughts make someone die?

Did Cory do anything wrong or bad to make (the deceased) die?

Did you do anything wrong or bad to make (the deceased) die?

Ana said, "Cory, you are doing a good job talking about difficult feelings. What other feelings do you sometimes have?" Cory said, "Sometimes I feel worried more bad things will happen. I feel worried (the caregiver) will go away and never come back. I hold on tight to (the caregiver) so they won't go away. All these worried feelings make my tummy hurt. And sometimes I have scary dreams."

Is Cory worried more bad things will happen?

What else makes Cory feel worried?

What makes you feel worried?

Ana explained to Cory, "It's normal to feel worried sometimes. It's normal to have scary dreams. You can turn your scary dreams into happy dreams. Draw a picture of a scary dream. Then draw a happy ending to the dream."

Does Cory have scary dreams?

Draw a picture of a scary dream. Then draw a happy ending to the dream.

Dear Caregiver,

This chapter focuses on emotional reactions typically experienced by grieving children. The purpose is to help children understand that their feelings and reactions to the death are normal and to provide them with appropriate coping strategies. Here are some issues we covered:

Sadness

Cory's Story normalizes feelings of sadness and conveys the message that it is okay to cry. **You can help** your child by normalizing sad feelings and giving permission to cry and to talk openly about sadness. For example, "This is a sad time for our family. It's okay to cry when we feel sad. Let's talk about your feelings—what do you feel most sad about?" Although it is difficult to see your child in pain, and you might think it's best to try to take away their sadness, it's more helpful to listen, validate feelings, and provide physical comfort. This approach helps children openly express themselves and learn that they can handle difficult emotions.

Some children act as if nothing has happened. There can be many reasons for this. The child may not fully understand that the person is dead and not coming back; children grieve in small doses and their sadness might pass unnoticed; and children may express grief in other ways such as clinginess, aggression, or regression (e.g., baby talk, bedwetting, or toileting accidents).

Don't be afraid to cry in front of your child or to openly express your sadness, as this will help your child's grief process. However, since some children feel anxious when they see their caregiver looking very sad or crying, it's important to reassure your child by saying "Even though I am sad, I am okay and I can still take care of you."

Guilt

It is common for children to blame themselves for the death. Children need to know that nothing they did or said caused the death. **You can help** your child by reiterating "nothing you said or did made (the deceased) die."

Worry

Bereaved children tend to have more worries. They may worry their caregiver will leave and never come back, or they may be concerned about who will take care of them. They may worry that other bad things are going to happen. Their worry might be expressed through behaviors such as separation anxiety or clinginess. Your child might have new fears (e.g., of the dark, monsters) or complain of stomach aches. You can help by repeatedly reassuring your child. For example, "I am going out for a little while but I will be back soon," "I am healthy and expect to be here to take care of you for a very long time," "There will always be a grown-up to take care of you," and "I will do my best to keep you safe."

Anger

Everyone gets angry at times, but some children have difficulty expressing their anger in appropriate ways. They may express their anger through temper outbursts or aggression. Children need to know that it is okay to be angry but it is not okay to let out anger in hurtful ways.

In today's session, your child learned a calming strategy called Stop! Freeze! Cookie Breathe! If you and your child practice this daily (ideally at bedtime, when calm), you will both be more prepared to use it to manage angry feelings.

Once your child has mastered Robot-Ragdoll (learned in a previous session) and Stop! Freeze! Cookie Breathe! they can choose the relaxation strategy they like best. Giving your child choices will empower them and will increase their motivation to use a healthy coping strategy.

Grieving children often feel overwhelmed by a mix of feelings. This can lead them to act out in different ways. **You can help** your child by praising them often. This will help to counter any bad feelings that your child may have. If your child is misbehaving a lot, you may feel like it's hard to praise them. However, when you regularly praise your child's desirable behavior, their behavior improves. The Brag Book is a simple technique that will help you praise your child more consistently. Here's how to do it:

- Get a notebook and keep it beside your child's bed.

- Praise your child's desirable behavior by using labeled praise. Labeled praise means telling your child exactly what they're doing that you like. For example: *I like the way you asked nicely for a treat; I'm proud of the way you shared your toy with your friend; It looks like you put a lot of effort into cleaning your room; You calmed yourself when you felt angry, I am so proud of you!*

- Each night at bedtime, write in the Brag Book one positive thing that your child did that day, then read the brag statement to your child. Keep the brag statement brief and praise one behavior.

Since praise is most effective when given right after the positive behavior occurs, use labeled praise in that moment, and then reinforce the praise statement at night when you write in the Brag Book. For example, "Thanks for listening when I asked you to put your toys away. Tonight, I'm going to write in your Brag Book about your good listening!"

If you feel like you don't have the time or energy to do the Brag Book, or your child's behavior has been especially challenging and you're too frustrated to praise them, then remind yourself that spending about five minutes a day doing the Brag Book will eventually lead to better behavior, enhanced self-esteem, improved relationship with your child, and a more peaceful home!

Attached is a copy of the chapter from today's session so you can better understand what was covered.

Chapter Overview
Telling the Story

(**Important note:** This chapter is for children with traumatic grief who are experiencing death-related trauma responses. It is essential to be well trained in exposure techniques before implementing the trauma narrative with children.)

Goals
- Reduce avoidance associated with the trauma
- Manage intrusive and upsetting trauma-related imagery
- Reduce distressing reactions related to the death, including anger, guilt, and/or posttraumatic stress reactions

Materials
- Child's scrapbook
- Markers or colored pencils
- Variety of toys/dolls/miniature figurines
- Camera
- Tape
- Two copies of "Telling the Story" (one copy for the child's scrapbook, one copy for the caregiver)
- Letter for the caregiver

Guidelines and Process Issues

Children with traumatic grief often experience intrusive images related to the death. They may try to avoid thinking or feeling about the person who died or the circumstances of the death. Children experiencing traumatic grief may have unhelpful or unhealthy thoughts and feelings about what happened, such as self-blame. They are often fearful and on guard for danger. These responses make it difficult for them to think about the person who died, which they must do if they are to accomplish the tasks of grieving and move on in a healthy way.

Trauma narration is an exposure technique. Exposure is an important component of many trauma treatments for children and adults. Through creating a trauma narrative, children talk about their memories of traumatic events (as well as what they are thinking and feeling about those events) while in the presence of a neutral, calm, and supportive therapist. This process helps the child feel heard and validated and desensitizes the child to the overwhelming feelings and memories associated with the trauma. Trauma narration also enables the child to discuss their thoughts and feelings about the events, providing an opportunity to correct cognitive distortions and make positive meaning of their trauma. For children experiencing traumatic grief, desensitizing them to trauma reminders enables them to think about the person who died and accomplish the tasks of grieving.

The trauma narrative should be initiated only after the child has developed sufficient affective regulation and coping skills and severe psychiatric or behavioral problems have been stabilized.

Using toys and play materials offers children a developmentally appropriate method for telling their story. Children often lack the words to adequately describe their traumatic experiences, but they can show what happened. Using play materials to recreate their experiences allows for the external, concrete, and manageable representation of the trauma experience. Additionally, play reenactment facilitates desensitization to trauma memories through repeated visual reexposure in a safe, therapeutic environment.

Providing the child with a variety of appropriate toys, pretend people, and miniature figures will help them create a detailed narrative. The child should be told to use the toys/figures to show what actually happened or what they imagine happened (not what they wish happened). Each significant scene that the child creates with the toys/figures should be photographed.

As the child reenacts through play and verbalizes their trauma story, write the details in a story format. Write the child's exact words (do not paraphrase), and repeat them back to ensure accuracy. Once the narrative is completed, place the story in the child's scrapbook, along with the accompanying photographs. This ensures that the child has a visual and concrete representation of the trauma narrative, and it facilitates the processing of the story. This will also assist the child in later sessions if the narrative is shared with their caregiver.

The trauma narrative takes several sessions, depending on the child's level of comfort with talking about the person who died and the circumstances of the death, and typically includes the following parts: before, during, and after the death, and the worst moment. The last part of the narrative focuses on eliciting positive, empowering feelings.

Complex trauma refers to traumatic events that are chronic, interpersonal, and occur within the context of caregiving relationships. The term also describes the symptoms associated with such experiences (Kliethermes, Schacht, and Drewry, 2014). When a child has experienced multiple traumas, constructing and processing the trauma narrative requires an extended approach that accounts for the cumulative nature of their experiences, emphasizing not just the events themselves but also the relational dynamics, range of emotions, and pervasive impact on the child's developing sense of self and worldview. The trauma narrative can be in the form of a timeline, which helps the child unjumble their trauma memories and have a more organized understanding of their experiences (while also highlighting positive memories and hope for the future). Or the trauma narrative can be divided into overarching themes rather than focusing on details of each traumatic incident.

The child should initially tell the story with few interruptions. Then further details can be elicited through open-ended questions, such as the ones below (adapted from Cohen et al., 2017, and Salloum, 2015).

Introduction
- Begin by telling all about you. Say your name, how old you are, and some of the things you like to do. (Choose one of the pretend people to be you, then use it to show me all about you and the things you like to do.)
- Say who you live with, their names, and some of the things you do together. (Choose pretend people for each of them, then use the pretend people to show me some of the things you do together.)
- Tell about the person who died. Say their name and how they were important to you. Tell some things about them like their favorite things to do. (Choose one of the pretend people to be the person who died.)

Before the death
- What did you like doing with (the deceased) before they died? Where did you like to go together? What was the most fun time? (Show me with the pretend people/toys some of your special times together.)

During the death
- Tell about the day the person died or when you heard that they died. (Show me with the pretend people/toys.)
- Where did the person die (e.g., at home, at school/work, outside somewhere)? (Show me with the pretend people/toys.)
- Tell about what happened the day the person died. (Show me with the pretend people/toys.) If you were not there to see what happened when the person died, tell about who told you what happened and what they told you about the day they died. (Show me with the pretend people/toys what you were told happened or what you think happened.)
- Who else was there and what were they doing? (Show me with the pretend people/toys.)
- What did the person say or do right before or as they were dying? (Show me with the pretend people/toys.)
- How do you think the person felt right before or as they were dying? (Show me with the pretend people/toys.)
- When it was happening, what did you do or say? What did you want to do or say? (Hold the pretend person that's you and tell what you did or said, or what you wanted to do or say.)
- What were you thinking when it was happening /right after it happened? (Hold the pretend person that's you and tell what you were thinking when it was happening.)
- What were you feeling when it was happening /right after it happened? (Hold the pretend person that's you and tell what you were feeling when it was happening.)
- What happened next? (Show me with the pretend people/toys.)
- Tell me more about it. (Show me with the pretend people/toys more about what happened.)
- Tell me again the part about ... (Show me again with the pretend people/toys the part about ...)
- Were there any rescue people or helpers? What did they do and say? (Show me with the pretend people/toys what the rescue people were doing and saying.)
- What did your ears hear when it was happening? (Hold the pretend person that's you and tell what your ears heard when it was happening.)
- What did your nose smell when it was happening? (Hold the pretend person that's you and tell what your nose smelled when it was happening.)
- What else do you want to say about what happened? (Show me with the pretend people/toys.)
- What or who helped you on that day? (Show me with the pretend people/toys.)

Worst moment
- What was the worst moment (the hardest, scariest, yuckiest)? (Show me with the pretend people/toys.)
- How upset are you feeling now after showing me the hardest or scariest moment (no upset feelings, a little upset, a lot upset)?

After the death
- If you went to the viewing/visitation/funeral/burial, what do you remember about it? What was the hardest part about the viewing/visitation/funeral/burial? How did you feel during it? What feelings did you see other people showing there and what was that like for you? Was there anything that helped you feel better at the viewing/visitation/funeral/burial?
- How has it been for you since the person died? (Show me with the pretend people/toys.)
- How has it been for other people in your family since the person died? (Show me with the pretend people/toys.)

- What do you miss most about the person who died? (Show me with the pretend people/toys.)
- What big changes have happened since the person died (like moving to a new home, different adults taking care of you) and how do you feel about these big changes? (Show me with the pretend people/toys.)
- If the person who died was here now, what do you think they would do to help you, or what would they say to you to help you feel better? (Show me with the pretend people/toys.)

The ending to my story
- What are some of your brave or proud moments since the person died? (Show me with the pretend people/toys.)
- What advice would you give to other grieving children that would help them? (Tell me what to write.)

Use clinical judgment when formulating questions that are appropriate to each child's unique situation. As the child responds to questions, make note of unhelpful or inaccurate cognitions that will be processed in future sessions. Also take note of statements suggesting helpful thoughts, meaning making, or positive coping. There will be opportunities to reinforce and build on those elements in future sessions.

Do not collude with the child's avoidance or reluctance to gloss over the most distressing aspects of what happened. Encouraging statements can help the child move forward with their story (e.g., "I know it's really hard to talk about the way the person died, but I know you're ready to talk about the scariest, worst parts, and I'm here to listen").

Validate the child's feelings, reinforce their strength, and communicate openness to bear witness. While it is difficult to see a child in emotional distress, remember that an important goal of gradual exposure is to create discomfort so the child can better manage overwhelming feelings and reactions.

The child's favorite coping strategy learned in a prior session (e.g., Robot-Ragdoll or Stop! Freeze! Cookie Breathe!) can be incorporated at the beginning and end of each session so they begin the narrative and leave the session in a calm state. If the child becomes overly distressed during the telling of the story, they can take a break to do a relaxation exercise, then return to the trauma narrative once the anxiety level is stabilized. This not only calms the child but also conveys the message that they can manage upsetting reactions.

Some children will be reluctant to talk about the death. This can be due to a number of factors, such as feeling it is too scary to talk about, feeling guilt about what happened, feeling unsafe to open up, lacking the words to verbalize their thoughts and feelings, worrying about being judged, protecting others from sadness, being told by others not to discuss the details, or avoiding memories of the trauma (Treisman, 2021).

Ensuring the child feels safe and empowered is a critical element to their willingness to openly discuss the death. Being curious and asking exploratory questions may help to determine the child's underlying reluctance:

- What are you worried might happen if you tell me the details of the death?
- Is there anyone who will be upset with you if you tell me the details of the death?
- How might you feel if you talk about the details of the death? Do you think you might feel scared, embarrassed, guilty, or maybe even have a bunch of different feelings?
- How do you think I might react if you tell me the details of the death?

Several strategies can be employed to engage children who are reluctant to complete the trauma narrative. Ideas include saying "I know it's difficult to talk about what happened, but I believe that you're ready to tell me your story, and I am ready to hear it"; affirming that nothing bad will happen if they talk about what happened; and sandwiching between fun activities (e.g., "We will play a fun game, then spend some time on your story, then you get to choose something fun to do"); and spending additional time on calming activities (e.g., breathing exercises, mindfulness video).

The benefits of the trauma narration should have been explained to the caregiver during the feedback session. However, reiterate this information at this stage. It is also helpful to predict for the caregiver that the child may resist attending sessions or may display an increase in trauma responses while the trauma narrative is being created. The caregiver's anxieties should be addressed at this point, and they should be praised for their continued commitment to bringing the child to sessions.

Once the child has started creating their trauma narrative, it is usually helpful to share it with the caregiver during their individual session (rather than waiting for the narrative to be finished). Gradually reading the trauma narrative to the caregiver improves their capacity to tolerate hearing the child's description of the event and strengthens their capacity to support their child. The caregiver's feelings and reactions to the child's trauma narrative must be carefully processed.

Conjoint sessions in which the child shares their narrative with their caregiver can occur when the child and caregiver are ready and have been appropriately prepared. The child should be prepared for this conjoint session well in advance so the sharing of the narrative does not come as a surprise. The caregiver must demonstrate an ability to provide appropriate emotional support to the child and be able to manage their reactions and emotions while hearing the child's account.

Before the conjoint session, a meeting can be scheduled with the caregiver to review specific statements that support the child during the reading of the narrative. Role-playing potential scenarios with the caregiver, and providing them with sample responses can be especially helpful—for example, "I know it may be hard for you to share your story with me, and it may be hard for me to hear it, but I know we can do it. We are both ready," and "I'm crying because it makes me sad to think about what happened. Even though it's really hard to talk about when (___) died, we can both handle it."

At the beginning of the conjoint session, implement an engaging activity, such as the Guess Which Hand Game, to put the child and caregiver at ease and to facilitate open communication.

If it is clinically contraindicated for the child to share the narrative directly with their caregiver, then conjoint sessions can focus on other issues, such as healthy coping strategies. It is also possible for the child to share only a small portion of the narrative with their caregiver, such as the content on what the child has learned as a result of experiencing the event or what they might tell other grieving children.

Telling the Story

Welcome back to the story! Ana said, "Today you're going to tell a very special story. It's a special story because it's all about you! Your story will have happy parts, like about the fun things you like to do, and sad parts, like about your (the deceased) who died. You can use toys and pretend people to help you tell your story." Cory interrupted Ana and said, "I'm excited to tell my story, but I don't want it to have any sad, bad parts." Ana said, "Lots of children don't like talking about sad, bad things that happened. But telling your story and talking about the death is a helpful way to cope with your feelings so you can eventually feel better. Don't worry, we will start with the easier parts to talk about so you get used to telling your story. We're not going to talk about any hard parts today. Today, I'd like you to use the toys/pretend people to tell me about you and about the fun things you like to do." Cory wanted to feel better. And Cory realized that telling about fun things was a good place to start the story!

You get to tell your own story too! Your story will have happy and sad parts. Your story will be about some of the fun things you like to do. Your story will also be about how (the deceased) died. I know you're ready to tell me your story, and to talk about happy and sad things that have happened.

You can use the toys/pretend people to help you tell your story. As you tell your story with the toys/pretend people, I will take pictures of what's happening, and I will write what you're saying so we can make a storybook. I'll ask you some questions to help you tell your story. You'll start your story today and continue the next time(s) that you come here.

Telling the Story

Dear Caregiver,

An important component of the healing process is helping your child create and discuss a story of the traumatic experience. This is called a *trauma narrative*. Creating the trauma narrative will help your child process frightening thoughts and feelings about the death. To help make the process easier for your child, the narrative is created a little at a time, beginning with easier parts, and gradually leading up to the more distressing parts. Your child will use toys to help them tell their story and to make the process more engaging.

As your child creates the narrative, I will pay close attention to your child's level of distress and pace the sessions appropriately. It is important that you let me know if you see any significant changes in your child's behavior at home, as this will help me assess how your child is responding to the development of the narrative. It would be particularly helpful to know if your child shows an increase in distress reactions, such as nightmares, difficulty sleeping, bedwetting, tantrums, or aggression. Don't be alarmed if you see an increase in any of these reactions for a time. This is normal as your child processes the trauma. **You can help** your child by giving them extra support and comfort. If you're having difficulty managing these reactions, please do not hesitate to let me know. We can set up a time to meet so I can provide added support to you and your child.

Your child may resist attending sessions at this point, as an attempt to avoid dealing with the trauma. **You can help** by encouraging your child to attend sessions. Try not to force or bribe your child to come to sessions. If there is a problem bringing your child, please contact me to consult.

Your child may ask you more questions about the details of the death. Answer any questions directly and honestly using simple language. If you are unsure how to respond, I am here to help!

As your child is creating the trauma narrative, you and I will also meet so I can share the story with you as it is being developed. Hearing your child's narrative may be very difficult for you. It is therefore important that you and I have an opportunity to meet without your child present so you can deal with your feelings and reactions and get the help and support you need. When you and your child are ready, we will meet all together so your child can share the narrative with you. The session with you and your child together will be conducted in a manner that ensures you both feel safe and supported.

Chapter Overview
Helpful Talk

Goals
- Identify unhelpful or inaccurate cognitions
- Replace maladaptive cognitions with more adaptive ones

Materials
- Child's scrapbook
- Markers or colored pencils
- Art supplies to make puppets
- Two copies of "Helpful Talk" (one copy for the child's scrapbook, one copy for the caregiver)
- Letter for the caregiver

Guidelines and Process Issues

Helping children to replace maladaptive cognitions with adaptive ones is a key coping strategy. Young children's thought patterns are just developing, so they are responsive to corrective information. This is important as unchallenged maladaptive thoughts can be detrimental to children. Encouraging adaptive thinking can lead to lifelong advantages in coping with adversity and supporting future success (Pollio & Deblinger, 2018).

Younger children lack the cognitive capacity to identify and correct maladaptive thoughts. However, they can learn adaptive self-statements. Using puppets to practice saying coping statements aloud makes the process more appealing and facilitates skill rehearsal and mastery. Simple puppets can be made from paper bags, paper plates, socks, and so on.

Once the puppets have been made, the "helper" puppet can ask the child's puppet questions to reveal possible cognitive distortions. For example, "How come (the deceased) died?" "Is there anyone or anything that could have stopped the death/saved the person from dying?" "What's a worry you have had since (the deceased) died?" "What would you say to another child whose (___) died to help them feel better?"

Some children have negative thoughts about non-death-related issues. For instance, they may assume that if they misbehave and get yelled at or punished, this means that their caregiver does not love them. Cognitive coping can help children learn skills to manage both death-related and non-death-related maladaptive thoughts.

Helpful Talk

Welcome back to the story! Cory came to see Ana with a sad look. Ana said, "Cory, you look sad. Tell me about your sad feelings." Cory replied, "Well, I was playing with my favorite toy, and then the worst thing happened. My favorite toy broke. Now I can't play with it anymore! I'm sad." Ana said, "Of course you're sad that your favorite toy broke. It's upsetting when something like that happens, but there are things you can do to make yourself feel better. One way you can make yourself feel better is by doing helpful talk. Helpful talk is what you say to yourself to feel better. So when your favorite toy breaks, if you say now I have nothing fun to do, this will make you feel sad. But if you say I have other fun things to do, this will make you feel better. Today I'm going to teach you how to do helpful talk so you can make yourself feel better. We're going to use puppets to help you learn to do helpful talk." Cory wanted to feel better so Cory was excited to learn how to do helpful talk. And Cory was excited to use puppets!

How did Cory feel when Cory's favorite toy broke?

Is helpful talk something Cory can do to feel better?

Is Cory excited to learn how to do helpful talk?

You also get to use puppets to learn helpful talk! First, let's make puppets. I will make a puppet to talk for me, and you will make a puppet to talk for you.

(Read after the two puppets have been made.)
Let's first use our puppets to talk to each other (use your puppet to ask the child's puppet the questions. Instruct the child to use their puppet to talk for them).

HELPER PUPPET:

Hi (child's name), how are you today? Tell me a little about you, like how old you are, and some things you like to do. (Use your puppet to engage the child's puppet in a brief, casual chat.)

Now that our puppets know each other better, let's use our puppets to do helpful talk. Let's pretend your puppet is upset. My puppet is the helper. My puppet will show you how to do helpful talk to make your puppet feel better. Then your puppet will copy what my puppet says. Like this:

CHILD'S PUPPET: My favorite toy broke.

HELPER PUPPET: I have other fun things to do.

CHILD'S PUPPET COPIES THE HELPFUL TALK: I have other fun things to do.

(From the scripts below, choose the ones that are appropriate for the child, or create new scenarios.)

CHILD'S PUPPET: There's no more cereal. I have nothing good to eat.

HELPER PUPPET: I can eat something else.

CHILD'S PUPPET COPIES THE HELPFUL TALK: I can eat something else.

CHILD'S PUPPET: I made a mistake. I have to start a new drawing.

HELPER PUPPET: It's okay for my drawing to have mistakes.

CHILD'S PUPPET COPIES THE HELPFUL TALK: It's okay for my drawing to have mistakes.

CHILD'S PUPPET: I'm worried my (caregiver) won't come back.

HELPER PUPPET: When my (caregiver) goes out, I know they will come back soon.

CHILD'S PUPPET COPIES THE HELPFUL TALK: My (caregiver) will come back soon.

CHILD'S PUPPET: I'm worried about who will take care of me.

HELPER PUPPET: There will always be a grown-up to take care of me.

CHILD'S PUPPET COPIES THE HELPFUL TALK: There will always be a grown-up to take care of me.

CHILD'S PUPPET: I sometimes feel scared.

HELPER PUPPET: When I feel scared, I can stay close to a safe adult.

CHILD'S PUPPET COPIES THE HELPFUL TALK: I can stay close to a safe adult.

CHILD'S PUPPET: I did something bad. Now my (caregiver) doesn't love me anymore.

HELPER PUPPET: Even when I don't listen or I break rules, my (caregiver) loves me no matter what.

CHILD'S PUPPET COPIES THE HELPFUL TALK: My (caregiver) loves me no matter what.

CHILD'S PUPPET: I did something bad to make my (deceased) get dead.

HELPER PUPPET: I didn't do anything bad to make my (deceased) get dead.

CHILD'S PUPPET COPIES THE HELPFUL TALK: I didn't do anything bad to make my (deceased) get dead.

CHILD'S PUPPET: I am worried that my (deceased) hurts or is in pain.

HELPER PUPPET: My (deceased) does not feel hurt/pain because a dead body does not feel hurt/pain.

CHILD'S PUPPET COPIES THE HELPFUL TALK: My (deceased) does not feel hurt/pain.

CHILD'S PUPPET: I don't feel safe. I'm scared.

HELPER PUPPET: I am safe right now.

CHILD'S PUPPET COPIES THE HELPFUL TALK: I am safe right now.

Dear Caregiver,

Grieving children often develop inaccurate or unhelpful thoughts related to the death. For example, they may blame themselves for the death or they may think that the world is an unsafe place. This chapter helps your child replace unhelpful thoughts with helpful thoughts (*called helpful talk*). Puppets are used to make the process easier and more appealing for your child. **You can help** your child by reinforcing the helpful talk.

You may also have inaccurate or unhelpful thoughts related to the death. We will discuss your thoughts about the death and ways you can replace inaccurate or unhelpful thoughts with accurate, helpful thoughts. Once you learn this coping strategy, you will feel better and you will be able to **help your child** identify more helpful or accurate ways to think.

Attached is a copy of the chapter from today's session so you can better understand what was covered.

Chapter Overview
Memories
(**Note:** This chapter may take more than one session to complete.)

Goals
- Identify and preserve positive memories of the deceased
- Normalize and verbally articulate ambivalent feelings toward the deceased

Materials
- Child's scrapbook
- Markers or colored pencils
- Die
- Photo book (created in advance by the caregiver; see guidelines below)
- Tape
- Two copies of "Memories" (one copy for the child's scrapbook, one copy for the caregiver)
- Letter for the caregiver

Guidelines and Process Issues

It is important for children to memorialize and remember the person who died not just immediately after the death but throughout their subsequent years. The concept of continuing bonds is characterized by the enduring emotional connection that bereaved individuals form with the deceased, integrating their memories and feelings into their day-to-day lives (Sirrine et al., 2018).

Bereaved children whose caregivers help them to feel connected to the deceased person experience more adaptive grief reactions (Alvis et al., 2022; Kaplow et al., 2014; Sandler et al., 2003.) Strategies to maintain a connection with the deceased include discussing memories of the deceased, sharing thoughts and feelings about mementos of the deceased, and memorial activities such as visiting the grave or participating in memorial services or rituals.

Young children may have difficulty recalling memories, so it can be helpful for them to look at family photographs and ask their caregiver to assist in recalling memories. Creating a book with family photos and short descriptions is one way to stimulate dialogue and encourage the sharing of memories and feelings. Since children have a limited attention span and may get restless while placing photos and descriptions in the book, it is best for the caregiver to create the book at home and bring it to the session to show to the child. The caregiver can be provided with guidelines for what to add to the book so that they include an appropriate assortment of photos but not so many that the book becomes overwhelming to the child. The descriptions that the caregiver adds for each photo should be brief and appropriate to the child's level of understanding.

It might be helpful for the photo book to include a page with photos of current significant others in the child's life who do things with the child that they miss doing with the deceased. For instance, if the child misses going to the park with the person who died, then the book can include a photo of who currently in the child's life takes them to the park. This can help the child commit to new or existing relationships, which is one of the tasks of grieving.

The last page of the book can include photos with short descriptions of the grave or urn (or area where the ashes were scattered), as this can help the child and caregiver talk about ways they can honor the memory of the person who died. The child and caregiver can also be encouraged to reflect on how they can hold onto their memories of the person who died or honor them on an ongoing basis. For example, in their living space, they can have framed photos of the person who died or they can engage in a favorite activity on the deceased person's birthday. Finally, the caregiver and child can identify any positive physical or personality traits that the child may have inherited from or share with the person who died.

Introduce the Dice Game after the child has looked through the photo book. The game is meant to captivate and maintain the child's attention and make the memorialization process more appealing. The game questions can be modified to suit the child's needs and circumstances. For children with limited attention spans, it may be more appropriate to divide the photo book and Dice Game into two sessions.

Looking at family photos can evoke strong emotions for bereaved families. Prepare the caregiver for this by meeting with them in advance of the session and discussing how they can cope with these emotions and, at the same time, support their child.

Children often focus only on positive memories of the person who died, fearing that speaking negatively of the dead will have detrimental consequences. However, an important goal with bereaved children is to process any negative or ambivalent feelings toward the person who died. These feelings toward the deceased may stem from conflict in the relationship (e.g., abuse, unresolved anger), shame or anger over the way the person died (e.g., substance-related death, gang-related death, suicide, drunk driving), or anger at perceived unnecessary death (e.g., did not seek medical care, did not wear seat belt). Discussion with the caregiver must occur before meeting with the child so they understand the rationale for talking about ambivalent feelings and can provide their child with permission to openly discuss any negative feelings and memories toward the deceased. As well, the caregiver may have insights about the deceased that can help the child process any ambivalent feelings that they have.

For younger children, consider having them make lists of "what I miss" AND "what I don't miss" about the person who died. Some younger children may lack the cognitive capacity to verbalize and work through any ambivalent feelings toward the person who died. Therefore, this issue may need to be revisited at a later stage in the child's development.

Memories

Welcome back to the story! Today we're going to talk about memories. Ana said, "Cory, when somebody dies, we can't see them alive again. We can't play with them again. We can't go places with them again. But we can look at photos of them. We can talk about the things we did with them. And we can remember them. What's something special that you remember doing with (the deceased)?" Cory said, "I remember going to the park together. We had so much fun on the swings and playing tag." Ana asked, "How do you feel when you remember this special time with (the deceased)?" Cory replied, "I feel happy because it's about a fun time!"

What's one of Cory's happy memories of the person who died?

Tell about one of your happy memories with your (deceased).

Ana said, "Cory, nobody is perfect, not even the person who died. Chances are, there are things you liked and didn't like about them. Tell about a sad or upsetting time with (the deceased)." Cory got an upset look and said, "Sometimes we used to fight. We both got angry and we yelled at each other." Ana asked, "How do you feel when you remember this time?" Cory replied, "I feel sad because it's about a bad time. And I feel like I shouldn't say anything bad about (the deceased)." Ana said, "Cory, like I said before, nobody is perfect. It's okay to remember and talk about both the good and the bad times."

What's one of Cory's sad or upsetting memories of the person who died?

Is it okay to talk about the sad or upsetting memories of the person who died?

Were there ever times when (the deceased) upset you or did things or said things that you didn't like? Tell me about those times. (You can tell or use the toys/pretend people to show the upsetting times.)

Tell about your worst memory of (the deceased). (You can tell or use the toys/pretend people to show your worst memory.)

How do you feel toward (the deceased) as you remember the upsetting times? (Remember, it's okay to have happy feelings and angry or upset feelings toward the person who died.)

Ana said, "Cory, like I said before, it's okay to have happy and sad feelings toward (the deceased). Now that we've talked about some of your sad, upset feelings, let's talk about some of your happy memories with (the deceased). We will look at photos of special times with (the deceased) to help you remember them."

Your (caregiver) brought photos to help us talk about your special memories. Let's look at the photos and talk about them.

(Read after the child has looked through the photo book.)
Let's play a game to help you talk about more memories. It's called the Dice Game. Roll the die. If you roll an even number (2, 4, 6) answer a question below. If you roll an odd number (1, 3, 5), choose one of the photos in your book and tell about it. Play until all the questions below have been answered. (I will write your answers to each question so you will never forget these memories.)

1. Tell about some fun things you did with (the deceased).
2. Describe some funny times together.
3. Tell about some nice things (the deceased) did for you.
4. Tell about something nice you did for (the deceased).
5. What are some things you miss doing with (the deceased)?
6. Say what you liked most about (the deceased).
7. Describe one of the best times ever with (the deceased).

(Read after playing the Dice Game.)
Looking at the photos made Cory feel happy and sad: Happy because it reminded Cory of the good times with (the deceased), and sad because it made Cory miss (the deceased) and the things they used to do together. Ana said, "Cory, it's normal to feel sad because you miss (the deceased) and the things you used to do together. There will be times when you feel sad, and there will be times when you feel happy and can laugh and play. When you miss (the deceased), it can help to know that your memories of them will last forever and ever! These happy memories will always be in your heart. Let's draw a heart. Then inside the heart, draw a picture (or glue a photo) of a favorite memory of (the deceased). When you look at this picture, it can remind you that your memories of (the deceased) are always in your heart!" Cory liked this idea!

You can do this too. Let's draw a heart. Inside the heart, draw a picture (or glue a photo) of a favorite memory of (the deceased). When you look at this picture, it can remind you that your memories of (the deceased) are always in your heart!

Dear Caregiver,

This chapter focuses on preserving memories of the person who died. Both negative and positive memories are discussed to help your child process any ambivalent feelings toward the person who died. **You can help** by giving your child permission to talk openly about any mixed-up feelings they have.

Talking about the person who died will stir up emotions—it's okay to show your feelings to your child, as this will help them grieve. Participating in activities that memorialize the person who died allows you and your child to preserve and honor their memory while providing a tangible outlet for their emotions. Below are some ideas:

- Place a photo of the person who died in a frame (or let your child choose the photo), and place the framed photo in your child's bedroom. (Or purchase an inexpensive wooden frame that your child can decorate before putting the photo in it.)
- Go around your home and neighborhood with your child and take photos of items that remind your child of the person who died. Place the photos (along with a short description) in your child's memory book. Use the photos to initiate discussion about the person who died.
- Make a Memory Jar: Together with your child, decorate the outside of a jar. Throughout the year, fill the jar with memories that come up of the person who died. On the anniversary of the death, read aloud the memories from the jar.
- Create a keepsake box with your child. Fill it with special items that belonged to the person who died. Look through the items in the box occasionally.
- Sew a pillow for your child out of a soft sweater that belonged to the person who died.
- Ask relatives and close friends to write a letter to your child sharing their special memories of the person who died.
- Make a video together in which you interview each other about your special memories of the person who died. Prepare a list of interview questions and interview other family members and friends about their special memories.

Chapter Overview
Wishes

Goals
- Normalize the hope that the person who died will come back
- Accept the finality of the death

Materials
- Child's scrapbook
- Markers or colored pencils
- Blanket or large towel (for the magic carpet)
- Two copies of "Wishes" (one copy for the child's scrapbook, one copy for the caregiver)
- Letter for the caregiver

Guidelines and Process Issues

It is common for children to fantasize that the person who died will come back. This may stem from the young child's limited understanding of the finality of death and their rich imagination and fantasy life. This may also be a coping strategy to avoid painful feelings and attempts to maintain life as they know it. Some children experience "magical thinking" in that they believe they have the power to bring the person back.

While it is normal for children to have some degree of magical thinking or hope that the person will return, persistent belief in this idea can interfere with their ability to navigate the grieving process and adapt to life without the person who died.

This chapter of *Cory's Story* and the Magic Carpet Ride offers appropriate support and guidance to help children come to terms with the reality of the death while providing them with the opportunity to process their emotions in a healthy way. A script is provided for the Magic Carpet Ride, but it can be modified. Creativity and an enthusiastic tone is encouraged!

The letter for the caregiver highlights the important role they play in helping their child accept the finality of the death. The letter also encourages the caregiver to validate the child's sadness and to reinforce healthy thoughts and positive meaning making.

Wishes

Welcome back to the story! Cory looked excited. Cory said, "It was my birthday yesterday. I got lots of presents and a yummy chocolate birthday cake with rainbow sprinkles, and guess what I wished for when I blew out the candles on my cake?" Ana replied, "Did you wish for all the toys in the world?" "No!" "Did you wish for a million dollars?" "No!" "I can't guess, what did you wish for?" asked Ana. Cory said, "I wished for (the deceased) to come back alive." Ana said, "Cory, sometimes children wish for things that might come true, and sometimes they wish for things that can never come true. Today we're going to talk about different kinds of wishes. To help us do that, we're going to go on a pretend magic carpet ride!" Wow, what fun, thought Cory!

We're going to go on a pretend magic carpet ride too! Hop on the special carpet. Pretend that it's a magic carpet! Listen carefully as I read the script for our magic carpet ride.

> This carpet is magic because it can fly. It's moving! We're flying up into the sky! Wheeee! We're flying through the air! What fun! Now the magic carpet is resting on a soft, cushy cloud. (Pretend to feel the soft, fluffy white cloud.) Look down there. (Point down.) I can see my house and the park. And look at all those cars! What do you see down there? (Allow the child to answer.)
>
> We're moving again. We're gently flying through the air. Hey, look at that flock of birds—we're flying as fast as them! (Wave to the birds.) Now we're flying down. Whoosh! We're landing! (Bump to a landing.) Now we're in The Land Where All Wishes Come True! Wow, look at this magical place! See the purple grass and the sparkly trees and the colorful rainbow and the butterflies made of gold? It's so amazing!
>
> In this very special land, all wishes come true, even super-duper crazy wishes come true! I wish for candy to fall from the sky! Poof! My wish came true! Look at all this candy ... Giant lollipops! Gummy bears! Caramels! Jelly beans! Now it's your turn to make a wish. What do you wish for? (Allow the child to answer.) This land where all wishes come true is so cool! I feel so happy here!
>
> Uh, oh! We're moving again ... We're going up! Whoosh! We're way up in the sky! We're gently gliding along. Feel the cool air on our face. Look over there, an airplane! (Wave to the people on the plane.) We're moving down, we're landing. Looks like we're back home. (Gently bump to a landing and get off.) We're back in my office/room. (Point out some things you see in the room.)

Ana said, "That magic carpet ride was pretty cool! It would be so wonderful if all our wishes came true, for real! But we were just pretending. In real life, all our wishes cannot come true. And that can make us feel sad. Like, I wish it could be my birthday every day so I could get lots of presents! Even if I wish really hard, I cannot make this wish come true. Lots of kids wish the person who died could come back alive. But when a person dies, their body stops working forever, and it can never be alive again. Even if we wish hard, the person who died cannot come back alive, not ever. Sometimes our wishes cannot come true." Cory knew Ana was right. Cory knew (the deceased) would never come back alive. This made Cory feel very, very sad.

Do lots of kids wish the person who died could come back alive?

When a person dies, can they ever come back alive?

How does Cory feel knowing that (the deceased) cannot come back alive?

How do you feel knowing (the deceased) can never come back alive?

All of a sudden, Cory thought of something. Cory said, "I've seen lots of movies. And in the movies, wishes come true. So maybe if I wish really, really hard, my wish will come true. My (deceased) will come back alive!" Ana replied, "Cory, it's different in the movies. Movies are not real. Movies are just pretend. So even if you wish really, really hard, your (deceased) cannot come back alive. It's normal and okay to feel sad, knowing that the person who died can never come back. When you feel sad, you can help yourself feel better by thinking of something happy. What is something that makes you feel happy?" Cory thought for a moment, then said, "I feel happy when I am coloring pictures. I love doing art!" Ana said, "When you feel sad or when you miss your (deceased), you can think of doing art, and this can help you feel better."

What makes Cory feel happy?

If Cory thinks of something happy, can this help Cory feel better?

What makes you feel happy?

Draw a picture of something that makes you feel happy. When you feel sad or when you miss the person who died, you can think of what makes you feel happy, and this can help you feel better.

Dear Caregiver,

Many children yearn for the person who died. Some children experience "magical thinking" in that they believe they have the power to bring the person back to life. When children remain stuck believing the person can come back, it can interfere with their healthy functioning. Once they realize the person is not coming back, they often feel overwhelmingly sad and powerless. This activity normalizes the sense of loss, reinforces the finality of the death, and empowers children to focus on the positive.

You play an important role in helping your child accept the finality of the death. **You can help** by reiterating the finality of death. For example, say "I wish (the deceased) could be here right now to see your play. I wish (the deceased) could come back. But I know (the deceased) cannot come back, not ever. This makes me feel very sad. How do you feel knowing (the deceased) cannot come back?"

It may be difficult for you to talk to your child about the finality of death in such a direct manner. It can be helpful to prepare for this discussion by anticipating the feelings you might experience such as sadness. Even though conversations like these can be difficult, know that you and your child will adjust better in the long run if these issues are addressed openly and you validate your child's feelings and offer emotional and physical comfort.

Your child drew a picture of something that makes them feel happy. When your child feels sad or has other difficult emotions, **you can help** by first validating their feelings, and then reminding them to think of the things that make them feel happy.

Attached is a copy of the chapter from today's session so you can better understand what was covered.

Chapter Overview
Coping with Hard Days

Goals
- Anticipate and cope with difficult days and future bereavement-related challenges
- Recognize that it is okay to feel sudden and intense surges of grief

Materials
- Child's scrapbook
- Markers or colored pencils
- Build-A-Teddy Bear template (included)
- Cardstock
- Scissors
- Envelope
- Tape
- Decorative craft supplies such as glitter glue, colored felt, stickers, etc.
- Two copies of "Coping with Hard Days" (one copy for the child's scrapbook, one copy for the caregiver)
- Letter for the caregiver

Advance Preparation
Photocopy the Build-A-Teddy Bear template onto cardstock. Cut the puzzle along the dotted lines and place the pieces in an envelope.

Guidelines and Process Issues
Prepare grieving children and their families for the likelihood that painful feelings will be reactivated at different times in the future, such as the anniversary of the death, birthdays, holidays and festivals, religious ceremonies, athletic events, special performances, important developmental milestones, a special song or storybook, and other significant events or loss reminders. These are called grief bursts.

This chapter helps the child and their caregiver prepare for grief bursts by planning what they will do to comfort themselves on difficult days. *Cory's Story* and the Build-A-Teddy Bear activity are developmentally appropriate interventions to help young children understand the concept of grief bursts and implement coping strategies. A variety of coping ideas are presented so the child can choose their preferred strategy.

This component is best accomplished via a conjoint session, coupled with an individual follow-up session with the caregiver to reinforce the important role they play in supporting their child through future challenges.

Coping with Hard Days

Welcome back to the story! Cory came to see Ana looking very upset. Ana said, "Cory, you look upset today. Tell me about your upset feelings." Cory replied, "It's my play tomorrow at school. I'm sad that my (the deceased) won't be there to see it. All the other kids will have their whole family there. And I won't. It's no fair! I'm sad and angry!" Ana said in a gentle voice, "Cory, it is very upsetting that your (the deceased) is dead and isn't here to be with you on special days like when you're in a school play. I can understand why you're sad and angry. There are times when you will feel sad and angry because you will miss your (the deceased). These are called grief bursts. There are special days that will be hard because your (the deceased) won't be with you. On these special days, you might feel happy if it's a fun day, and you might also feel sad, angry, or other upset feelings because you will miss your (the deceased)."

Does Cory feel sad and angry because (the deceased) isn't there to see the school play?

Is it normal to feel sad on certain days because you miss the person who died?

What are special days when you might feel sad because you will miss the person who died?

Ana said, "Cory, when you miss your (deceased), there are things you can do to cope with these hard days. Today we're going to do an activity called Build-A-Teddy Bear. It's a puzzle and a fun craft activity that will help you learn ways to feel better when you are upset." Cory liked doing puzzles and crafts, so Cory was excited for the Build-A-Teddy Bear activity.

You get to do the Build-a-Teddy Bear Puzzle and craft activity too! First, put the puzzle together, then I'll help you tape it on all sides.

(Read after the puzzle has been assembled.) Let's read the ideas written on the bear. You can draw a happy face beside the ideas you like best! Then you can decorate your teddy bear.

Take your teddy bear home and put it beside your bed. When you're feeling sad or upset, choose one of the ideas on your bear that will help you feel better.

Build-A-Teddy Bear

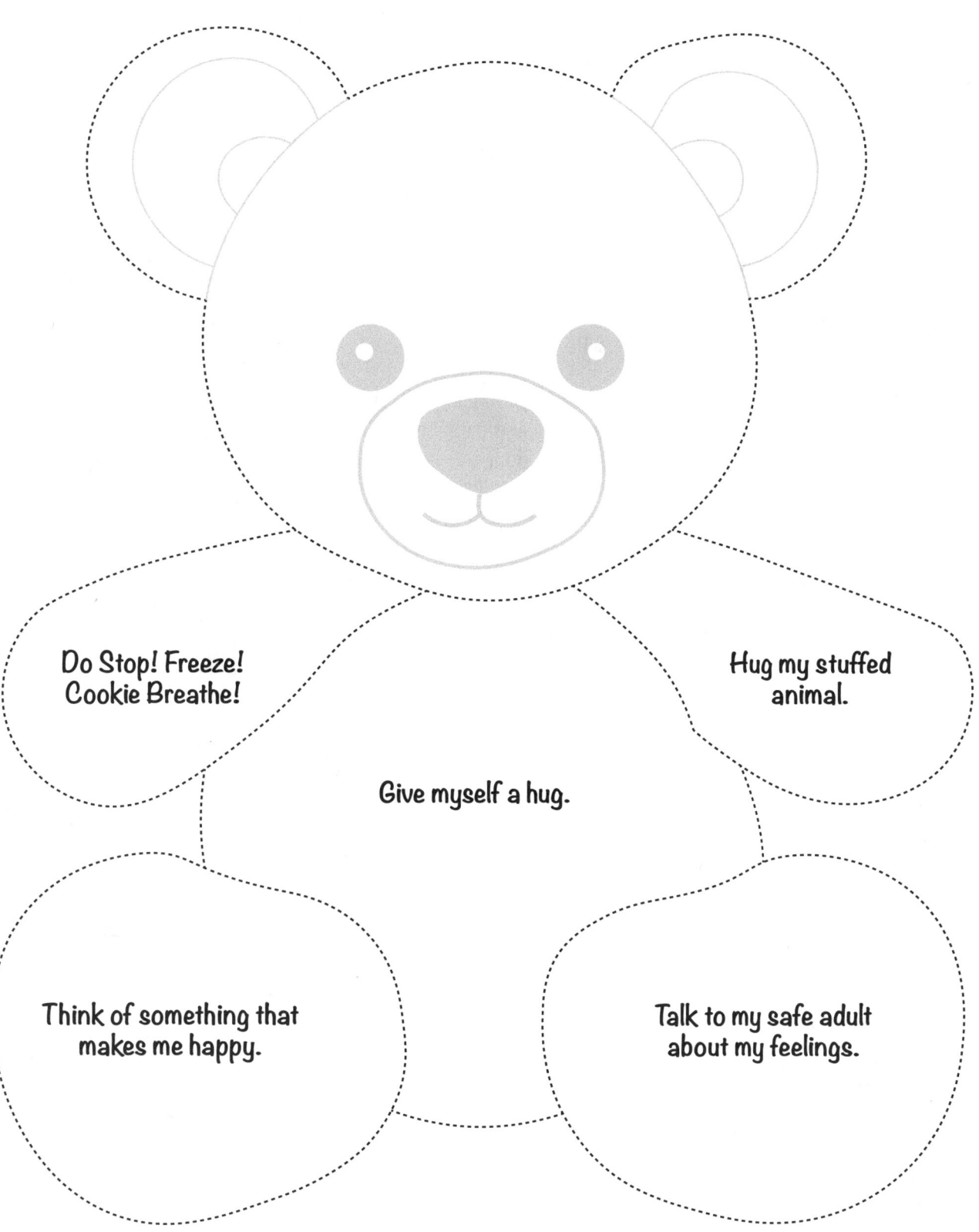

- Do Stop! Freeze! Cookie Breathe!
- Hug my stuffed animal.
- Give myself a hug.
- Think of something that makes me happy.
- Talk to my safe adult about my feelings.

Dear Caregiver,

Bereaved individuals do not get over their grief, but the painful emotions do lessen over time. People continue to grieve the death, although with lowered levels of intensity. Various events, such as the anniversary of the death date, family celebrations, and so on, are likely to intensify feelings for a time. These are called grief bursts. Grief bursts are a normal part of the grieving process.

Identifying potential difficult days ahead can help your child and family manage these situations. It is also important to be prepared for grief bursts that may not be connected to a trigger and just sometimes happen. Each time a grief burst happens, and you and your family get through it, you prove that you can manage it.

The Build-A-Teddy Bear activity can help your child cope when they feel sad or upset. **You can help** your child by coaching them to use an idea on the bear. Below are some additional ideas to help your child and family cope with grief bursts:

- Honor the person who died by eating their favorite meal, partaking in their favorite hobby, or listening to their favorite song.
- Plant a tree or some flowers in a place that holds special memories.
- On your child's birthday, write them a letter indicating how proud you are of them (be specific about some of your child's accomplishments from the past year). Include in your letter how proud the person who died would have been of your child.
- If the person who died was a parent, then Mother's Day/Father's Day may trigger a grief burst. Your child may feel sad, lonely, jealous, or angry on this day, especially when they see other children with their parent. Even though their mother or father has died, they are still their parent and your child may want to honor them by making a Mother's/Father's Day card. They can leave the card at the grave/where their ashes were buried/scattered or keep it in a special place. It may also be helpful to speak with your child's teacher to discuss ways they can support your child on Mother's Day/Father's Day and on other days that might be especially hard.

Special occasions and other times may bring a range of feelings and reactions. Your child may feel happy, sad, or a mix of emotions. It is important to accept whatever feelings your child expresses on these days.

Chapter Overview
Saying Goodbye

Goals
- Review and celebrate gains made in sessions
- Articulate an appropriate understanding of why sessions are ending
- Provide a positive goodbye experience

Materials
- Child's scrapbook
- Markers or colored pencils
- Questions for the Crumpled Paper Throw Game (included)
- Colored cardboard
- Two wood craft sticks
- Scissors
- Tape
- Craft supplies
- Two copies of "Saying Goodbye" (one copy for the child's scrapbook, one copy for the caregiver)
- Letter for the caregiver

Guidelines and Process Issues

Bereaved children often struggle with endings and goodbyes as their feelings of loss are reignited. The last session, therefore, must be handled with sensitivity and carefully planned well in advance. This can be a collaborative process with the caregiver. For example, the caregiver can bring to the last session a small celebratory treat.

The Cookie Jar activity (Appendix E) is geared especially to young children to help prepare them for the last session. As indicated in the Introduction/Theoretical Overview, it should be introduced when there are five sessions left.

The goals of the last session are to review and celebrate the successes and accomplishments made, reflect on the child's new abilities to cope more effectively, address feelings about ending, and provide a healthy model for saying goodbye.

The Crumpled Paper Throw Game is reintroduced to provide a sense of continuity. This version of Crumpled Paper Throw helps the child consolidate gains and can stimulate further discussion about issues learned in sessions. When playing the game, the child stands behind a designated throw line. Stand far enough from the child to make the game challenging but close enough to ensure the child has some success in throwing the crumpled paper through the hoop. Use opportunities throughout the game to praise the child's accomplishments in sessions.

The final chapter of *Cory's Story* normalizes the child's feelings about termination. The Goodbye Hand is a child-friendly intervention that facilitates the goodbye process. It becomes a transitional object for the child once sessions have ended. The message that is written on the hand to be given to the child should be succinct and include a positive message for the child's future. For example, "I wish you lots of smiley faces in your very bright future!" or "Congratulations on all your hard work! You are a super-duper kid and you deserve all the very best!"

The child's scrapbook can be given to the caregiver in the last session. The caregiver should keep the scrapbook in a place at home that ensures its privacy and safekeeping. The child and their caregiver can be encouraged to look through the scrapbook together in future years—for instance, on the anniversary of the death. This can be particularly helpful as many of the activities completed during sessions will have new meaning as the child approaches their grief differently in future developmental stages.

In some cases, it might be best to review the scrapbook with the caregiver in their individual session before giving it to them. If the scrapbook includes content that would be inappropriate to share with the caregiver, then use discretion about whether to send it home. Parts of the scrapbook can be given to them, especially those that will be helpful for the child to revisit in later years. (Note: Abide by professional policies and procedures regarding the storage of files, and if mandated, a copy of the child's scrapbook should be made for the file before giving it to the child.)

Saying Goodbye

Welcome back to the story! Today is a special day. Today is Cory's last day seeing Ana. Ana asked Cory, "How do you feel that today is your last day and you won't be coming back?" Cory answered, "I feel happy and sad. I feel happy because I got help from you and I feel much better now, but I feel sad because I like coming here and I will miss you." Ana said, "I enjoy being with you and I will miss you too. But I am glad that you got the help you needed. Sometimes it's hard to say goodbye to someone that you won't see again. But you can feel good knowing that when we say goodbye today, it's because you got the help you needed."

Is Cory ready to stop coming here because Cory got the help that Cory needed?

Are you ready to stop coming here because you got the help that you needed?

Cory feels happy and sad knowing today is the last time coming here. How do you feel knowing today is your last day and you won't be coming back?

Ana said, "Cory, before we do an activity that will help us say goodbye to each other, we're going to talk about some of the things you learned here. You learned what death means. You learned about feelings children may have when someone important to them dies. You learned ways to help yourself feel better. Today we're going to play Crumpled Paper Throw again, but this time when we play the game, we're going to focus on some of the important things you learned in here. Let's follow the instructions below to play the game." Cory was excited to play the game!

We're going to play the game too. Let's follow the instructions.

Crumpled Paper Throw Game

Crumple a piece of paper into a ball. Stand behind the line, and throw the paper ball toward the hoop I make with my arms. If you get the crumpled paper through the hoop, you get a high-five! If you miss, I will ask you a question. (The questions will help you talk about some of the things you learned here.) Let's play!

Questions: Crumpled Paper Throw Game

1. You learned what dead means. When a person dies, can they breathe, move, play, eat, or sleep?

2. You talked about your feelings about the death. Say two feelings you have had about the death.

3. You learned to do Robot-Ragdoll and Stop! Freeze! Cookie Breathe! Choose one, then do it now to show that you know how to help your body get calm and relaxed.

4. You learned to do helpful talk to make yourself feel better. If your favorite toy breaks, which one is helpful talk: "Now I have nothing fun to do" OR "I have other fun things to do."

5. You talked about happy memories of the person who died. Tell again about one of your happy memories of the person who died.

6. You learned that when a person dies, they can never come back alive, even if we wish really hard. Tell how you feel knowing that (the deceased) can never come back alive.

7. You did the Build-A-Bear Puzzle and learned ways to cope with hard days. When you are feeling sad or upset, what is something you can do to feel better?

(Read after playing the Crumpled Paper Throw Game.)

Ana said, "Cory, you did a great job talking about some of the important things you learned here. Now we're going to prepare to say our last goodbye to each other. It can be hard to say goodbye when you know you're not coming back here again. To make it easier to say goodbye to each other, let's each make a cardboard Goodbye Hand. Then we can use the cardboard hands to wave goodbye to each other when you leave here for the very last time today." Cory thought this was a great idea!

We're going to make Goodbye Hands too. Let's follow the instructions.

Goodbye Hands

We will each trace our hand on a piece of colored cardboard, cut out the hand, decorate and write on it a goodbye message to each other. (I'll help you with the tracing, cutting, and writing.) Then we will tape each cardboard hand onto a stick. When you leave here today, I will give the Goodbye Hand that I decorated to you and you will give the Goodbye Hand that you decorated to me.

(Read at the end of the session when it's time for the child to leave.)

Let's give each other the goodbye hand we made for each other and read the goodbye messages written on the hands. Then, as you are leaving here, we will use our Goodbye Hands to wave goodbye to each other.

Dear Caregiver,

You have already accomplished one of the most important ways to help your child—you have brought them to sessions so they were able to process the grief. **You can help** your child by initiating regular talks about feelings, engaging in activities together that memorialize the person who died, offering continued comfort and support, and reminding your child to use the coping strategies learned in sessions. **You can also help** your child by continuing to use the strategies that YOU learned in sessions, like Pillow Talk and the Brag Book.

Your child's scrapbook should be kept at home in a place that ensures its privacy and safekeeping. I encourage you and your child to look through the scrapbook together in future years—for instance, on the anniversary of the death. This can be particularly helpful as your child gets older and better understands some of the concepts that we covered.

As you and your child continue on your grief journey, there may be times when you need added support. There is always help available, including information online, self-help books, and organizations that support bereaved families. Accessing support when it is needed is one of the best ways **you can help** yourself and your child.

You and your child have persevered through hard times. You have both become emotionally stronger and better equipped to cope with life's difficulties. When you're in a challenging situation in the future, think about how you coped, persevered, and supported your child, and know that you and your child have the strength to get through anything.

Appendix A: Caregiver Questionnaire

CAREGIVER QUESTIONNAIRE

Date: _____ Person Completing Form: _____ Relationship to Child: _____

Child's Name: _____ Date of Birth: _____ Age: ___ Address: _____

Caregiver's Name: _____ Date of Birth: _____ Occupation: _____

Phone # (Cell): _____ Home #: _____ Email: _____

Caregiver's Name: _____ Date of Birth: _____ Occupation: _____

Phone # (Cell): _____ Home #: _____ Email: _____

Child's School: _____ Teacher: _____ Grade: _____ Phone #: _____

List all those living in your child's home:

Name	Relationship	Age/School/Occupation
_____	_____	_____
_____	_____	_____
_____	_____	_____
_____	_____	_____
_____	_____	_____

List other significant adults outside the home who are strong supports for you or your child:

_____

_____

What are your concerns about your child, and how are you hoping sessions can help?

_____

_____

Has your child been seen previously for grief support/mental health assessment or therapy? (If yes, indicate name of professional, date/place of service, for what purpose, and any diagnosis provided.)

_____

_____

Describe child's development (complications at birth, colicky, delays in development, other difficulties):

_____

_____

Appendix A: Caregiver Questionnaire

Other than the death, describe any serious life stressors your child has experienced (such as abuse, neglect, divorce, placement away from home, other stressful or frightening events):

_____
_____

Describe concerns raised by daycare/school about your child (emotional, behavioral, social, academic):

_____
_____

List any health concerns, ongoing medications your child is taking and describe for what purpose:

_____
_____

Date of the death and child's age at time of the death _____

Describe what your child's relationship was like with the person who died:

_____
_____

Circumstances of the death (how person died, anticipated/sudden, violent, if child witnessed the death or suffering, child's preparation for the death, other significant details)

_____
_____
_____
_____
_____
_____
_____

If the person died from a long-term illness, describe diagnosis, treatment, child's involvement in end-of-life stage, and impact on the child:

_____
_____

Appendix A: Caregiver Questionnaire

How did child initially learn about the death? (Witnessed? If notified afterward, who told the child, what was child told, how did child react?)

_____
_____

Describe your cultural/spiritual beliefs and practices about death, after death, child's involvement and reactions (viewing/funeral/memorial/ burial/cremation, other mourning rituals):

_____
_____

Is it easy or hard for you and your child to talk about the death? What questions has the child asked about the death and how have you responded? Does child avoid talking about the person who died?

_____
_____

Child's emotional presentation since the death (shows little emotion, cries a lot, angry outbursts, etc.)

_____
_____

Are there any people, places, or situations that remind your child of the death and frighten them? Does child avoid going places or doing activities that are reminders of the death/person who died?

_____
_____

Has child created keepsakes of the person who died or read books about grief? (Please describe):

_____
_____

Describe any family conflict related to the death/not related to the death:

_____
_____

What significant changes has child faced since the death and how have they reacted (moved, new school, separation from family, new caregiver)?

_____
_____

Appendix A: Caregiver Questionnaire

Please check-off if your child is experiencing any of the following, and elaborate:

Reaction/Behavior	✓	Please Describe
Talks about missing the deceased		
Has scary memories of the death		
Worries about bad things happening		
Is clingy or afraid to be alone		
Believes the death was their fault		
Has difficulty sleeping in own bed		
Has nightmares		
Startles easily, very jumpy		
Has difficulty concentrating or focusing		
Cries a lot, not enjoying daily activities		
Has frequent tantrums, aggression		
Has frequent stomach aches, headaches		
Has difficulty with peers, gets bullied		
Wets bed, soils self, withholds stool		
Is overly sensitive to sounds/clothing		
Gets easily upset when makes a mistake		
Says wants to die/hurts self on purpose		
Says doesn't like self or body		

Please describe any other reactions or behaviors you are concerned about or behaviors that your child is exhibiting that you find challenging to deal with:

_____

_____

Appendix A: Caregiver Questionnaire

Caregiver's Background (Each caregiver should complete a separate form; make additional copies if needed.)

Where were you raised and by whom? Describe past/current relationship with your parents:

_____
_____

Describe any of the following you experienced during childhood and how it affected you: death of close family member; physical/sexual abuse; neglect; spousal abuse; divorce; other significant stressors or trauma.

_____
_____

Describe the happiest time and the saddest time from your childhood:

_____
_____

Are there ways you try to be similar to your parents, or not like your parents?

_____
_____

Describe whether you or any family members have ever had any of the following:

Serious illness: _____

Depression/bipolar disorder: _____

Anxiety disorder: _____

Obsessive-compulsive disorder: _____

Learning disability/ADHD: _____

Eating disorder: _____

Substance misuse: _____

Criminal activity/conviction: _____

Have you been seen previously for grief support/mental health assessment or therapy? (If yes, indicate name of professional, date/place of service, for what purpose, and any diagnosis provided.)

_____
_____

Appendix A: Caregiver Questionnaire

On a scale of 1-10, how are you coping since the death (0 = Not well, 10 = Very well): _____

What has been most difficult for you since the death?
_____
_____

What has helped you the most since the death?
_____
_____

Please add any other information about your background that you feel is important:
_____
_____
_____
_____
_____
_____
_____
_____
_____
_____
_____
_____
_____
_____
_____
_____
_____
_____

Appendix B: Family Assessment Activity

Playdough Adventure
Materials: Playdough

Instruct the family as follows: "I would like each of you to create an animal using the playdough. Give your animal a name and introduce your animal to me. Then pretend that the animals are going on an adventure together. Talk with one another about where the animals are going on their adventure. A problem happens on the adventure—you get to decide what the problem is. The animals are very clever because they come up with a good idea to solve the problem. Show me with your playdough animals what happens during this adventure. Show what happens at the beginning of the adventure, then show me what happens during the adventure when the problem happens, and then show me what happens at the end when the animals come up with a good solution to solve the problem."

At the end of the play, ask the following questions (talk to the animals rather than to the humans, and modify the questions as needed):

1. What was it like to be your animal?
2. How did the animals get along?
3. How did it feel when the animals had the problem?
4. Who came up with the solution to the problem?
5. Did all the animals agree on the same solution to the problem or did they have a fight/disagreement about it? If there was a fight, how was this handled?
6. What feelings did your animal have during the adventure?
7. What did you like/not like about the adventure?

Appendix C: Sample Welcome Letter for the Child's First Session

Date: _____

Dear _____,

You are here today because someone important to you died. It is normal to have upset, mixed-up feelings when someone dies. This is a place where children come to get help with their upset feelings and learn ways to feel better. You may feel nervous or scared about coming here today, but hopefully you'll feel better as we get to know each other.

Each time we meet, we will do some talking and some playing. I'll choose activities for us to do first, and then you get to choose what to do.

The activities we do here will be put in this special book. I will keep your special book for now. When you come here for the last time, I will give you your special book to keep.

Let's take a picture of you for the cover of your special book.

I look forward to talking and playing with you!

From,

_____

Appendix D: Child Assessment Activity

Red or Black Card Game
Materials: Standard 52-card deck, Get Moving Grab Bag (See next page)

This game will help me get to know you better. It's called the Red or Black Card Game. Pick the top card from the deck of cards. If it's a <u>red card</u>, answer the question. If it's a <u>black card</u>, pick a card from the Get Moving Grab Bag. We will both follow the instructions on the card from the Get Moving Grab Bag. Play until all the questions below have been answered.

1. What is your favorite color?
2. What is your favorite toy to play with?
3. Make a <u>happy</u> face. Then say something that makes you feel happy.
4. Make a <u>sad</u> face. Then say something that makes you feel sad.
5. Make a <u>scared</u> face. Then say something that makes you feel scared.
6. What makes your (caregiver) feel sad, angry, or upset?
7. What do you know about when, where, and how (the deceased) died?
8. Who helps you when you have a problem or worry? How do they help?
9. Tell about something fun you got to do.

Appendix D: Movement Activity

Get Moving Grab Bag
Materials: Scissors, small gift bag

Cut out each of the movement activities below and place them in a bag.

Jog on the spot for 5 seconds, then take 3 deep breaths.	Do 3 jumping jacks, then take 3 deep breaths.
Jump forward, then back, then take 3 deep breaths.	Jump up and down 3 times, then take 3 deep breaths.
Touch your toes, then take 3 deep breaths.	Tap your nose 3 times, then take 3 deep breaths.
March in place 10 times, then take 3 deep breaths.	Tap shoulders 3 times, then take 3 deep breaths.
Hop for 10 seconds, then take 3 deep breaths.	Clap 5 times, then take 3 deep breaths.
Do big arm circles 5 times, then take 3 deep breaths.	Give yourself a hug, then take 3 deep breaths.

Appendix D: Child Assessment Activity

People in My World

Materials: Yellow, blue, purple, green, black, and red markers, People in my World template (See next page)

(**Note**: Guide the child to include themselves and the most significant people in their world, including positive and negative relationships.)

This activity will help you talk about the important people in your world. The first step is to fill in the picture of the world by writing the names of the important people. Write the name of each person in a different section of the world (I will do the writing). Include yourself, the people you live with, other people in your family, adult relatives you spend a lot of time with or who help take care of you like grandparents, aunts, uncles, and your teacher. Add other important people you feel especially close to or who have really hurt/upset you and you still think about this hurt. Next, add how everyone feels:

Draw yellow happy faces on anyone who feels happy a lot. How come they're happy?

Draw blue sad faces on anyone who feels sad a lot. How come they're sad?

Draw purple X's on anyone who feels angry a lot. How come they're angry?

Draw green X's on anyone who feels scared a lot. How come they're scared?

Draw black X's on anyone who did something very wrong or very bad. What did they do that was very wrong or bad?

Draw red hearts on anyone who helps you when you have a problem or worry. What do they do to help you?

Appendix D: Child Assessment Activity

People in My World

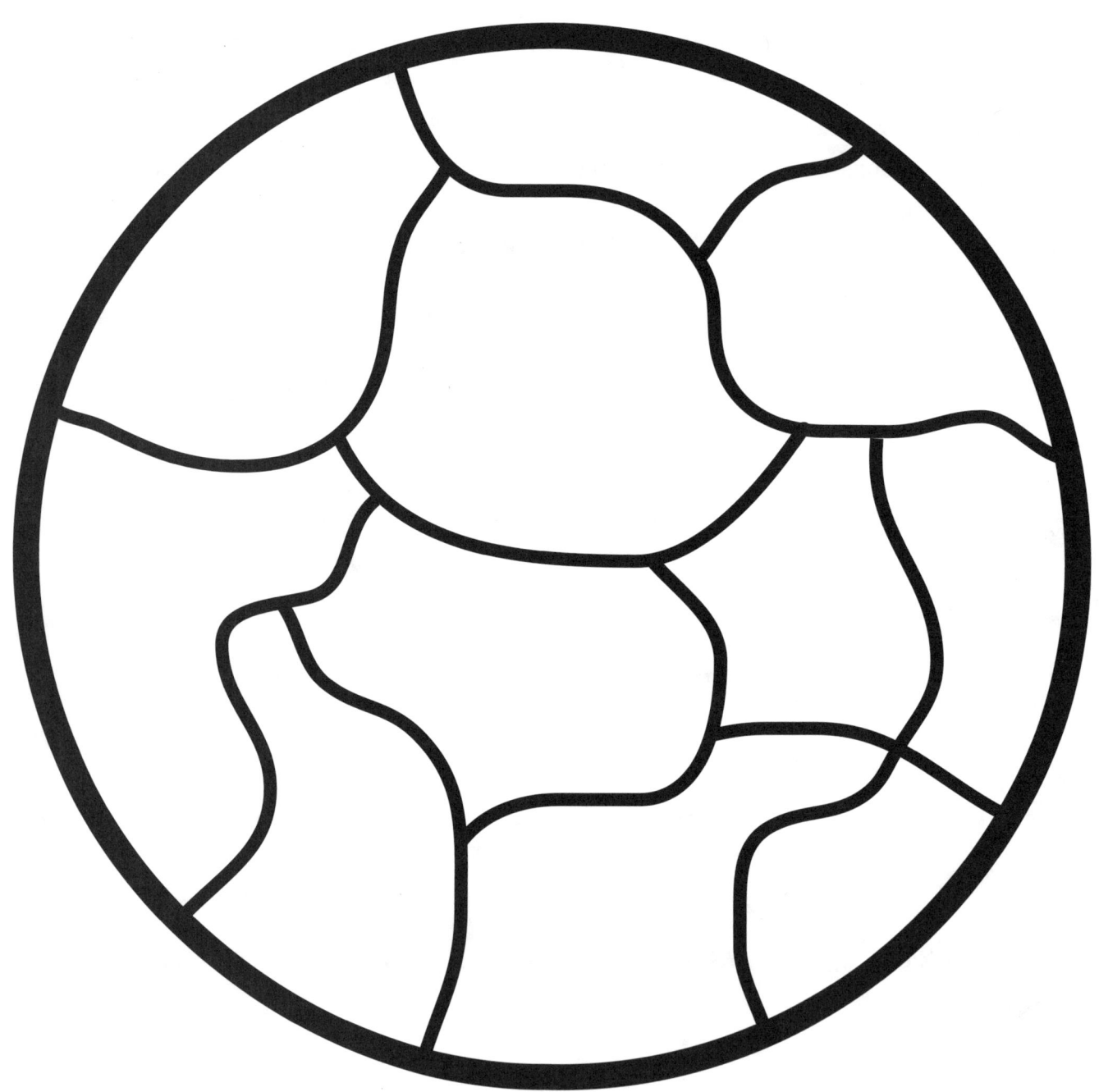

104

Cookie Jar

Materials: Plastic covered jar or container, adhesive label, marker, five cookies

(**Important note:** This activity prepares the child for the last session. Ideally, it should be introduced when the child has five more sessions. Prepare the activity before the session by writing the child's name on the adhesive label and sticking it on the outside of the jar. Place the five cookies in the jar and close the lid. As an alternative to actual cookies, five printable cookie templates that the child colors can be printed from the internet. Modify the activity if paper cookies are used.)

You have done a great job talking about your feelings and learning ways to feel better! This means you are almost ready to stop coming here. This activity is called Cookie Jar. It will help you understand why you are almost ready to stop coming here.

Open the cookie jar, take out one cookie (only one!), and eat the cookie. The remaining cookies in the jar show how many more times you will be coming here. There are four cookies left in the jar. So you will be coming here four more times, and then you and I will be saying goodbye to each other. Place the lid on the cookie jar.

Ask me to say some of the important things you have learned here and to explain why you are almost ready to stop coming here.

We'll do this activity again at the end of our next three sessions (eat one cookie from the cookie jar, count the remaining cookies in the jar, and say how many more times you will be coming here). At the end of the three sessions, there will be one cookie left in the cookie jar, which means you will come here one last time. The last time you come will be a time for us to say a last goodbye to each other. We will do a special activity the last time you come to help us say a last goodbye to each other. At the end of your last session, you will get to eat the last cookie left in the jar.

References

Avis, L., Zhang, N., Sandler, I., & Kaplow, J. (2022). Developmental manifestations of grief in children and adolescents: Caregivers as key grief facilitators. *Journal of Child and Adolescent Trauma*. https://doi.org/10.1007/s40653-021-00435-0

American Psychiatric Association. (2022). *Diagnostic and statistical manual of mental disorders* (5th ed., Text rev.).

Arnold, C. (Ed.). (2018). *Understanding child and adolescent grief: Supporting loss and facilitating growth*. Routledge.

Bierman, K. L. (1983). Cognitive development and clinical interviews with children. In B. B. Lahey & A. Kazdin (Eds.), *Advances in clinical child psychology* (Vol. 6, pp. 217–250). Plenum Press.

Blin, C., & Jonas-Simpson, C. (2018). Understanding trauma and grief complications. In C. Arnold (Ed.), *Understanding child and adolescent grief: Supporting loss and facilitating growth* (pp. 34-46). Routledge.

Cavett, A.M., & Drewes, A. (2012). Play applications and trauma-specific components. In J. Cohen, A. Mannarino, & E. Deblinger (Eds.), *Trauma-focused CBT for children and adolescents: Treatment applications* (pp. 105–148). Guilford Press.

Cohen, J. A., & Mannarino, A. P. (2011). Supporting children with traumatic grief: What educators need to know. *School Psychology International*, 32(2), 117–131.

Cohen, J. A., & Mannarino, A. P. (2019). Trauma-focused cognitive behavioral therapy for childhood traumatic separation. *Child Abuse & Neglect*, 92, 179–195. https://doi.org/10.1016/j.chiabu.2019.03.006

Cohen, J. A., Mannarino, A. P., & Deblinger, E. (2017). *Treating trauma and traumatic grief in children and adolescents* (2nd ed.). Guilford Press.

Doka, K. (Ed.). (1989). *Disenfranchised grief: Recognizing hidden sorrow*. Free Press.

Edgar-Bailey, M., & Kress, V. E. (2010). Resolving child and adolescent traumatic grief: Creative techniques and interventions. *Journal of Creativity in Mental Health*, 5(2), 158–176. https://doi.org/10.1080/15401383.2010.485090

Freedy, J. (2018). Understanding trauma and grief complications. In C. Arnold (Ed.), *Understanding child and adolescent grief: Supporting loss and facilitating growth* (pp. 107–122). Routledge.

Gil, E. (2015). *Play in family therapy* (2nd ed.). Guilford Press.

Goldman, L. (2014). *Breaking the silence: A guide to helping children with complicated grief—Suicide, homicide, AIDS, violence, and abuse* (2nd ed.). Routledge.

Goldman, L. (2022). *Life and loss: A guide to help grieving children: Classic edition*. Routledge.

Grant, R. J. (2023). *The AutPlay therapy handbook: Integrative family play therapy with neurodivergent children*. Routledge.

References

Griese, B., Burns, M., & Farro, S. A. (2018). Pathfinders: Promoting healthy adjustment in bereaved children and families. *Death Studies, 42*(3), 134–142.

Haine, R. A., Ayers, T. S., Sandler, I. N., & Wolchik, S. A. (2008). Evidence-based practices for parentally bereaved children and their families. *Professional Psychology, Research and Practice, 39*(2), 113–121. https://doi.org/10.1037/0735-7028.39.2.113

Harris, D. L., & Bordere, T. C. (2016). *Handbook of social justice in loss and grief: Exploring diversity, equity, and inclusion*. Routledge.

Harris, D. L., & Winokuer, H. R. (2016). *Principles and practices of grief counselling* (2nd ed.). Springer.

Kaplow, J. B., Layne, C. M., & Pynoos, R. (2014). Parental grief facilitation: How parents can help their bereaved children during the holidays. *Traumatic Stress Points*.

Kaplow, J. B., Layne, C. M., Pynoos, R. S., & Saltzman, W. (2023). *Multidimensional grief therapy: A flexible approach to assessing and supporting bereaved youth*. Cambridge University Press.

Kaplow, J. B., Saunders, J., Angold, A., & Costello, E. J. (2010). Psychiatric symptoms in bereaved versus non-bereaved youth and young adults: A longitudinal epidemiological study. *Journal of the American Academy of Child and Adolescent Psychiatry, 49*(11), 1145–1154. https://doi.org/10.1016/j.jaac.2010.08.004

Keyes, K. M., Pratt, C., Galea, S., McLaughlin, K. A., Koenen, K. C., & Shear, M. K. (2014). The burden of loss: Unexpected death of a loved one and psychiatric disorders across the life course in a national study. *American Journal of Psychiatry, 171*(8), 864–871. https://doi.org/10.1176/appi.ajp.2014.13081132

Killough-McGuire, D., & McGuire, D. E. (2001). *Linking parents to play therapy*. Routledge.

Kliethermes, M., Schacht, M., & Drewry, K. (2014). Complex trauma. *Child and Adolescent Psychiatric Clinics of North America, 23*(2), 339–361. https://doi.org/10.1016/j.chc.2013.12.009

Knell, S. M., & Dasari, M. (2006). Cognitive-behavioral play therapy for children with anxiety and phobias. In H. G. Kaduson & C. E. Schaefer (Eds.), *Short-term play therapy for children* (pp. 22–50). Guilford Press.

LaVigne, M. (2020). *Play therapy activities: 101 play-based exercises to improve behavior and strengthen the parent-child connection*. Rockridge Press.

Lieberman, A. F., Padron, E., Van Horne, P., & Harris, W. W. (2005). Angels in the nursery: The intergenerational transmission of the benevolent parental influences. *Infant Mental Health Journal, 26*, 504–520.

Lowenstein, L. (2006). *Creative interventions for bereaved children*. Champion Press.

Lowenstein, L. (Ed.). (2008–2022). *Assessment and treatment activities for children, adolescents, and families: Practitioners share their most effective techniques* (Vols. 1–4). Champion Press.

Lowenstein, L. (Ed.). (2010). *Creative family therapy techniques: Play, art, and expressive activities to engage children in family sessions*. Champion Press.

Lowenstein, L. (2016). *Creative CBT interventions for children with anxiety*. Champion Press.

Mellenthin, C. (2019). *Attachment centered play therapy*. Routledge.

National Child Traumatic Stress Network. (2016). *Children with traumatic separation: Information for professionals*. https://www.nctsn.org/sites/default/files/resources/children_with_traumatic_separation_professionals.pdf

Pearlman, L. A., Wortman, C. B., Feuer, C. A., Farber, C. H., & Rando, T. A. (2014). *Treating traumatic bereavement*. Guilford Press.

Perry, B. D., & Hambrick, E. P. (2008). The neurosequential model of therapeutics. *Reclaiming Children and Youth*, 17(3), 38–43.

Pollio, E., & Deblinger, E. (2018). Trauma-focused cognitive behavioural therapy for young children: Clinical considerations. *European Journal of Psychotraumatology,* 8(Suppl. 7), 1433929. https://doi.org/10.1080/20008198.2018.1433929

Rabenstein, S. (2018). Assessing grief and loss in children and adolescents. In C. Arnold (Ed.), *Understanding child and adolescent grief: Supporting loss and facilitating growth* (pp. 19–33). Routledge.

Salloum, A. (2015). *Grief and trauma in children*. Routledge.

Sander, I. N., Ayers, T. S., Wolchik, S. A., et al. (2003). The Family Bereavement Program: Efficacy evaluation of a theory-based prevention program for parentally bereaved children and adolescents. *Journal of Consulting and Clinical Psychology*, 71(3), 587–600. https://doi.org/10.1037/0022-006X.71.3.587

Sandler, I. N., Wolchik, S. A., Ayers, T. S., Tein, J. Y., & Luecken, L. (2013). Family bereavement program (FBP) approach to promoting resilience following the death of a parent. *Family Science,* 4(1). https://doi.org/10.1080/19424620.2013.821763

Schuurman, D., & DeCristofaro, J. (2010). Children and traumatic deaths. In D. Balk & C. Corr (Eds.), *Children's encounters with death, bereavement, and coping* (pp. 257–269). Springer.

Shapiro, D. N., Howell, K. H., & Kaplow, J. B. (2014). Associations among mother-child communication quality, childhood maladaptive grief, and depressive symptoms. *Death Studies*, 38(1–5), 172–178. https://doi.org/10.1080/07481187.2012.738771

Shear, M. K., Boelen, P. A., & Neimeyer, R. A. (2011). Treating complicated grief converging approaches. In R. A. Neimeyer, D. L. Harris, H. R. Winokuer, & G. F. Thornton (Eds.), *Grief and bereavement in contemporary society: Bridging research and practice* (pp. 139–162). Routledge.

Sirrine, E. H., Salloum, A., & Boothroyd, R. (2018). Predictors of continuing bonds among bereaved adolescents. *Omega*, 76(3), 237–255. https://doi.org/10.1177/0030222817727632

Sori, C. (2006). *Engaging children in family therapy: Creative approaches to integrating theory and research in clinical practice*. Routledge.

Spooner, C. (2021). *Attachment-focused family play therapy: An intervention for children and adolescents after trauma*. Routledge.

Stroebe, M. S., Hansson, R. O., Schut, H., & Stroebe, W. (2008). Bereavement research: Contemporary perspectives. In M. S. Stroebe, R. O. Hansson, H. Schut, & W. Stroebe (Eds.), *Handbook of bereavement research and practice: Advances in theory and intervention* (pp. 3–25). American Psychological Association. https://doi.org/10.1037/14498-001

Substance Abuse and Mental Health Services Administration. (2014). *SAMHSA's concept of trauma and guidance for a trauma-informed approach.* HHS Publication No. (SMA) 14-4884.

Treisman, K. (2021). *Ollie the octopus: Loss and bereavement activity book.* Jessica Kingsley Publishers.

Villarreal-Davis, C., Watts-Figueroa, C., & Turner, R. (2021). Serving together: Play therapy to foster attachment in grieving military families. *International Journal of Play Therapy*, 30, 231–243. https://doi.org/10.1037/pla0000168

Van Dijk, I., Boelen, P. A., de Keijser, J., & Lenferink, L. I. M. (2023). Assessing DSM-5-TR and ICD-11 prolonged grief disorder in children and adolescents: Development of the Traumatic Grief Inventory–Kids–Clinician-Administered. *European Journal of Psychotraumatology*, 14(2), 2197697. https://doi.org/10.1080/20008066.2023.2197697

Warnick, A. L. (2015). Supporting youth grieving the dying or death of a sibling or parent: Considerations for parents, professionals, and communities. *Current Opinion in Supportive and Palliative Care*, 9(1), 58–63. https://doi.org/10.1097/SPC.0000000000000115

Watts-Figueroa, C., & McCallum, A. R. (2023). The sacrifice of service: Grief and loss within the military community. In R. Blocker Turner & S. D. Stauffer (Eds.), *Disenfranchised grief: Examining social, cultural, and relational impacts.* Routledge.

Worden, J. W. (1996). *Children and grief: When a parent dies.* Guilford Press.

Organizations and Resources

Association for Death Education and Counseling: www.adec.org

Children and Youth Grief Network: www.childrenandyouthgriefnetwork.com

Child Bereavement UK: www.childbereavementuk.org

Coalition to Support Grieving Students: www.grievingstudents.org

Dougy Center: www.dougy.org

Eluna: www.elunanetwork.org

Grief Australia: grief.org.au

HealGrief: www.healgrief.org

Judi's House/JAG Institute: judishouse.org

KidsGrief: www.kidsgrief.ca

Mygrief: www.mygrief.ca

National Alliance for Children's Grief: nacg.org

National Child Traumatic Stress Network: www.nctsn.org

Our House: www.ourhouse-grief.org

Resilient Parenting for Bereaved Families: www.bereavedparenting.org

Tragedy Assistance Program for Survivors: www.taps.org

What's Your Grief: whatsyourgrief.com

Winston's Wish: www.winstonswish.org

FREE BONUS GIFT

As a purchaser of this book, you're entitled to a **bonus gift!**

Download the eBook:

**Favorite Therapeutic Activities
for Children, Youth, and Families:
Practitioners Share Their Most
Effective Interventions**

This eBook is a creative collection of assessment and treatment techniques for individual, group, and family sessions.

To download the free eBook and to get more resources including articles on cutting-edge topics, featured techniques, and links to YouTube videos, go to:

www.lianalowenstein.com